To Peggy

2/16/20

Saint Vincent Martyr Parish:

FROM CHURCH TO COMMUNITY

FINBARR M. CORR, ED.D.

On the cover:
(from left to right)
Rev. Edward Holterhoff, M.A.,
Rev. Finbarr M. Corr, Ed.D.
Rev. Joseph Fortuna

Saint Vincent Martyr Parish:
FROM CHURCH TO COMMUNITY

Corr, Finbarr M.
www.finbarrcorr.com

ISBN-13: 978-0-578-21431-3

FMC PRESS INC.
8918 Cranes Nest Court
Fort Myers, FL 33908
finbarrcorr@comcast.com

DEDICATION

*This book is dedicated to my wife
Laurie Hutton-Corr, and to her sister
Mary Woodward, for their guidance and support.*

Thanks to my fellow writers on Cape Cod - the Rising Tide Writers (RTW) - for their insights and criticism as I drafted this book during the past year.

Thanks also to my friend and fellow author Tom O'Connell for his sensitive review printed on the back cover.

TABLE OF CONTENTS

Saint Vincent Martyr Parish:

FROM CHURCH TO COMMUNITY

INTRODUCTION

My readers over the years are wondering how I, an Irish-born priest, ended up becoming pastor of a distinguished parish in New Jersey whose members were sixty percent Italian. I didn't apply for it and when the bishop called me on that Monday morning in 1979, while we at the Family Bureau Office were celebrating my tenth anniversary as director of the agency, the only clue he gave me was "Finbarr, you are exactly what they need right now."

I had been ten years removed from ministry in a parish and still had fond memories of my favorite pope at that time, Pope John XXIII, who opened the windows of the Church, initiating Vatican Council II (1962-65). The Church was no longer the male hierarchy but the *"People of God."*

When I moved from Saint Margaret of Scotland parish in Morristown, NJ in 1969 to become the first full-time director of the Family Life Bureau, I had this unconscious sense that if I ever became pastor of a parish, I would create a Post Vatican II parish in honor of Pope John XXIII.

I knew Father Joseph Fortuna very well but had never met the second associate pastor at Saint Vincent's, Father Edward Holterhoff. All I knew was that he had been a student at the Gregorian University in Rome and was ordained in Rome for the Diocese of Paterson NJ. Fortunately, they both accepted the concept of creating a pastoral leadership team.

They selected two younger lay trustees to who managed the finances. Father Joe choose Livvy Dinneen to become our youth minister and together, according to Livvy, we created a Saint Vincent Martyr Parish "Camelot."

CHAPTER 1

A Surprise Phone Call

On May 7, 1979, we had our usual weekly staff meeting at the Family Life Bureau office in Paterson, New Jersey. All of our staff - three therapists, a Family Life Educator, one secretary and me, the director - were still on an emotional high.

A few months earlier we had celebrated an extraordinarily successful Family Day Rally at Rutgers Stadium in New Brunswick. Our ecumenical Board of Governors, along with the Family Life Directors from the three other New Jersey dioceses and 1,500 volunteers, had chipped in to make the first statewide Family Day a huge success.

Father Frank, our popular marriage and family therapist, arrived at the meeting 10 minutes late. Instead of apologizing for his tardiness, he sat down, gave me a great big smile, and said. "Boss (he liked calling me Boss), I congratulate you and wish you a happy tenth anniversary as director of the Family Life

Bureau. You started this agency 10 years ago admittedly, with the support of my vote on the Personnel Board. You've had a very limited budget from the diocese; but, working with us here as your staff, you created the best agency in the diocese." I thanked him, of course.

Frank was not finished. He then gave me a serious, determined stare as he continued. "Boss, you have been working very hard for all these years. Those of us who've been here for many of those years know the hours you spend counseling couples and families, serving on weekends, preaching at all the masses in different parishes . . . it's never-ending."

He paused for a moment and added, "Boss, I am proposing to the whole team that you take May, June and July off. We will pick up your schedule of counseling and preaching. You don't have to notify the Chancery Office." Looking down at the table, he was silent as he waited for my answer.

I admit I was very moved by Father Frank's offer. I knew he was a truly fraternal priest who didn't want me to kill myself working.

I replied, "Let me think about it and I will get back to you in a couple of days." As the meeting ended and we returned to our offices, I was seriously thinking of either going home to Ireland for three months or visiting my older sister Marie and her husband Jack in Carlsbad, California.

An hour later Diana Rodriguez, our secretary, called me on the intercom to say that Bishop Rodimer (my boss) was waiting to speak to me on the phone. I wondered who the hell had told him it was the tenth anniversary of my appointment to Family Life? It was Bishop Casey who had appointed me in 1969, so how did Rodimer know? This was my second surprise of the day.

"Hello, Bishop" I said.

"How are you, Finbarr?" he replied in a friendly voice that told me I was not in any trouble.

I replied, "Fine, Bishop. To what do I owe the honor of a call from your lordship on Monday morning?"

He chuckled a little and said, "I am in upstate New York at a meeting with my fellow bishops. I took a break to ask you a personal question."

There was an awkward pause. I didn't have a clue what he was going to say. I was tempted to joke with him and say, "Thank you, Bishop, for remembering my tenth anniversary in Family Life."

Before I could speak, he asked, "Finbarr, how would you feel if I appointed you pastor of St. Vincent Martyr Parish in Madison?"

I replied impulsively. "Bishop, Madison is full of Italians. How do you think I would manage there with my Irish brogue?"

"I believe you are exactly what the parish needs right now," he said with conviction.

I thought about his offer for a few days and asked the Holy Spirit to guide me in making the right decision. I had long believed that 10 years in any one assignment was enough. I didn't want any community to feel they owned me. Secondly, I also felt that Bishop Rodimer was showing me a lot of respect by offering me the position of pastor of one of the most prestigious parishes in the diocese.

On Thursday morning I called the chancery office to accept the offer.

When the bishop replied to my "Good morning," his tone was different than when he had called on Monday. An experienced therapist, I could interpret the tone of an individual's voice immediately. His voice didn't have the same excitement about my possible leadership of St. Vincent's.

I ignored my suspicion and replied, "Bishop, I would be happy to accept your appointment of me as pastor of St. Vincent's."

He paused a moment and then said, "Finbarr, first you will have to interview with the priests' Personnel Board at Valley Road in Clifton. May I tell them that you can meet them this coming Monday at 10 AM?" I agreed.

After my Irish-brogue comment, I supposed he was uncertain that I would accept the position. When I reported the conversation to my colleague Father Frank, he smiled and said, "It is too bad that I am no longer a member of the Personnel Board. With all you have achieved in the past years, I don't know of any priest the board will recommend over you."

I was quite relaxed as I entered the personnel office on Monday morning.

If I didn't get the job, I would be comfortable serving as Family Life director for another couple of years.

The three priests sitting at the table gave me a warm welcome. Two of them were younger than me. The third was older and had served in the chancery office as director of personnel for a few years. The younger priests appeared nervous, possibly because they had to ask questions of an older priest, one who was also popular as the leader of the Family Life Bureau and who had recently coordinated a highly publicized and successful Family Day Rally.

The one question from the director of priest personnel surprised me. He asked, "Finbarr, how do you visualize your role as leader of St. Vincent's parish?"

I impulsively replied, "I see myself as more of a team leader who shares authority with the two associate pastors and, over time, also with the lay leaders in the parish." The two younger priests seemed surprised at my response. When I explained my rationale for team ministry, they became more relaxed. I believed I had won them over.

The interview lasted 45 minutes. I thanked them and exited from a different door than the one I had entered. As I turned to close the exit door, I recognized that another priest - one I knew - was entering. Now I realized why Bishop Rodimer's attitude toward me had changed between Monday and Thursday. He had another priest competing for the job.

When I returned to the Family Life office, both Father Frank and our secretary Diana had mixed feelings. Frank was certain I would win over any other applicant for the position, but both he and Diana hated the thought of losing me as their boss and friend after ten happy and hard-working years of our work together for families of the diocese.

We didn't have to wait long for the news from the priests' personnel office. The director called me on Friday morning at 11AM to announce, "Congratulations, Finbarr. Bishop Rodimer has appointed you pastor of St. Vincent Martyr Parish in Madison effective June 1, 1979. You will receive an official letter next week."

CHAPTER 2

Leaving Family Life

Whether it is good news or bad news, diocesan news travels at the same speed. My first phone call was to my spiritual director Father Andrew, a Benedictine monk. He agreed to meet the following morning, after I had offered my usual 7 AM mass for the five nuns in the provincial house in Paterson.

I didn't share the news with the nuns until we sat down for breakfast. I knew that telling them before mass would be a distraction. As I finished eating my toast and fried eggs, I announced, "Sisters, I have a surprise for you."

Three of the four nuns started laughing. They were accustomed to my Irish humor and expected some joke. The provincial superior remained serious and stared at me.

This time I repressed my Irish humor and simply said, "Sisters, Bishop Rodimer has appointed me as pastor of St. Vincent Martyr Parish in Madison. I will need your prayers, as I, an Irish-born priest, am taking over from a pastor who was born in Madison. How do you think a community where 10% were born in Italy and 40% are of Italian descent will accept an Irishman, who, I am told, still speaks with a brogue?"

They all smiled, including the provincial, and said in unison, "St. Vincent's is very lucky."

The most stressful phone call that week was to my older brother, Father Jack, who was pastor of Christ the King Parish in New Vernon, New Jersey. He had already heard the news. He said dryly, "(Father) Steve Patch told me, and he is very disappointed. He had hoped to get the St. Vincent's appointment as his last parish assignment before he retires."

That response didn't bother me. It confirmed that Bishop Rodimer's decision was a compliment to the leadership skills he felt I had. I wanted to ask Jack how he felt about it, especially since St. Vincent's was next door to Christ the King, but I decided not to add to the already substantial sibling rivalry between us.

The staff at the Family Life office had mixed feelings about my departure. They felt happy that my new appointment was an honor, but they worried about who would replace me.

I tried to lighten the mood at the next staff meeting. As I came down the stairs and joined them, Father Frank, on time for a change, was sitting there without his usual smile. I looked at him casually and asked, "Frank, do you want me to call Rodimer and tell him that you are ready to take over and direct the Family Life Bureau?"

Everyone laughed except Frank. He lowered his head and said with some passion, "Boss, while I am professionally prepared to take over counseling your clients and your other duties, I don't have the skills to coordinate Family Day rallies or to do all the fundraising you do with the ecumenical Board of Governors. Thank you for your kind offer."

"Okay, Frank, I will hire you as a weekend assistant at St. Vincent's after I get organized. I would like to continue the friendship we have built over the years."

"Thanks, Boss," he replied with a bit more energy.

As I expected, the Social Committee headed by my good friend Shirley and our secretary Diana (Dee) organized a retirement party at a local church auditorium. The members of the Board of Governors and all 150 volunteers were invited. Father Frank, who served as Master of Ceremonies, had also invited several of my fellow priests to attend. Needless to say, they all had a fun evening roasting and toasting the guest of honor.

Jesse Barton, that year's president of the Board of Governor's gave an emotional and moving presentation on my achievements as Director of the Family Bureau over ten years. He got a good laugh when he announced, "Father Finbarr is going to go to Italy for six months to learn Italian. I hope his new parishioners in Madison will understand his Italian spoken with an Irish brogue."

Even though I had visited the more than 100 parishes in the Diocese of Paterson in my role as director of the Family Life Bureau and knew most of the priests, I didn't know much about the culture of St. Vincent Martyr parish. I had also served as a therapist of nuns and priests for several years, so I had to be careful not to break the confidences that both priests and nuns shared with me. The job I was leaving certainly had memorable moments. One of my primary jobs when I started in September 1969 was to initiate Education in Human Sexuality (commonly called Sex-Ed) in all the Catholic grammar schools of the diocese. With the support of my boss

Bishop Lawrence B. Casey and volunteer Dr. Claude Coutinho, we made good progress in spite of resistance from the Roman Forum, a conservative group who opposed our purpose.

Sometimes Roman Forum members would picket or attend our meetings. They nicknamed me the "Sex Priest." I once went to the men's room before such a session and discovered, while at the urinal, that there was an informal meeting of the Roman Forum in process right behind my back.

One gentleman said quite loudly, "I wasn't planning to attend until I heard that the Sex-Priest Corr was speaking tonight."

Still turned to the wall, I said in a loud voice, "Sir, if you will wait until I am finished here, I will join your meeting." They all scurried like scared rats out to the auditorium. Our team decided to skip the question-and-answer session that evening.

A few years later, an older nun came to my office for counseling. A younger nun accompanied her. As the elderly nun struggled up the stairs, she stopped at the top and asked, "You are not related to that Sex-Priest Corr, are you?"

I winked at the younger sister and replied to the older nun, "No way sister, he is crazy."

During the weeks leading up to my move to St. Vincent's parish, I heard reports about significant dissension between the pastor and several traditional families in the parish. Without sufficient consultation with parishioners, the pastor had apparently decided to completely rearrange the inside of the church. His redo removed the main altar, transferred the tabernacle, and added a modern marble altar and new seats without kneelers. Parishioners especially disliked the new light pendant that shone down on the mass celebrant and altar servers. Some of the parishioners refused to donate to the refurbished church, and the family that donated the main altar requested its return to them.

I began to suspect that serving as the new pastor of St. Vincent Martyr Parish might be even more challenging than organizing a Family Day rally of 18,000 people. I called a colleague who was a pastoral associate in Madison and jokingly asked, "Are the people of Madison ready to have an Irish-born therapist as their pastor? Bishop Rodimer believes that I am exactly what the parish needs right now."

He laughed and replied, "You won't believe this! One parishioner wants to know if you spend a lot of time on the golf course and at the racetrack, like many of your Irish colleagues."

CHAPTER 3

The Influence of Vatican Council II

I was ordained on June 11, 1960 and began my priestly ministry in the Diocese of Paterson, New Jersey in August 1960. In 1958 the Papal Conclave had elected Pope John XXIII, an Italian cardinal who was already 76 years old. This was a great surprise to me, and a shock to most of the priests and hierarchy in the global Church. We expected that, given his age, the new pope would be an inactive stopgap pope who would merely occupy the papal seat until a more qualified and younger candidate came along.

He proved us wrong. On October 11, 1962, Pope John announced that he was convening Vatican Council II. He was summoning the Catholic cardinals of the world, along with selected bishops and theological experts, to convene at the Vatican to renew the Church and make it more relevant at a time when the world was experiencing the most accelerated social change in human history.

When Pope John issued this summons to Rome, I was 27 years old with only two years of experience as a parish priest. I was, however, aware enough to recognize that the practice of offering the mass in Latin, especially in the United States, was no longer relevant in the 1960s.

A fellow author, Father James Mallon, describes the situation at that time in his book *Divine Renovation: Bringing Your Parish from Maintenance to Mission*:

> "Demographics supported our pastoral development through the birth of children and the movement of migrants. We just had to build it and people would come. I do not believe we were particularly good at making disciples 50 years ago, but it was not obviously to our detriment. If we would go and open churches, there were always new communities of migrants and new babies. As we baptized and taught in our schools, we pumped out good 'practicing Catholics'. In a sense, we got away with not making disciples, because our culture propped it all up."[1]

I grew up in Ireland as the child of parents who were devout practicing Catholics. When my parents talked about the Church back then, they were referring to the Church hierarchy, the cardinals, bishops and priests. They never felt or were taught that, since they were baptized, they were also an important part of the Church as the people of God.

Vatican Council II must have confounded them. The Council dramatically redefined the relationship between the pastor and the parish. As a newly ordained priest in the inner city of Paterson, New Jersey, I was excited about the possible changes in the Church's liturgy and practices. Unlike many older and introverted priests, I was an extrovert who had not liked celebrating mass with my back to the congregation. I did not enjoy saying the introductory part of the mass in Latin - Introibo *ad altare Dei* (I will go unto the altar of God) - and praying in a language the congregation didn't understand.

Reading reports about the Council in the *National Catholic Reporter*, I realized the Church didn't belong to those of us who were the priests and the male hierarchy. Our role as priests was to invite laypeople in our parishes to become disciples of Christ and to teach them how to minister to each other, building up the Church as the body of Christ.

I believed that the call to all of us to be evangelizers began during Vatican Council II, which lasted from 1962 to 1965. The council produced sixteen documents, each a synthesis of an original Catholic doctrine, taught and practiced over the centuries and now revised by the council fathers to include the universal call to holiness and to mission.

In 1966 I was transferred to Saint Margaret of Scotland parish, a suburban parish in the town of Morristown, New Jersey. My new boss, Monsignor Christian Haag, trusted my ability to preach and evangelize the parish. He teased me, "Finbarr, you read the Scriptures on Sunday morning as if you wrote them yourself." He also encouraged me to drive 55 miles each week to Iona College in New Rochelle New York, to study psychology and to obtain a M.S. degree in Pastoral Counseling.

While stationed in Morristown, I was invited by my good friend Ann Logan to participate in Living Room Dialogues with members of other Christian churches in town. Animated by the spirit of Vatican Council II, I met monthly with members of the High Church and Low Church Episcopalians, Methodists, Baptists, (both American and African American), and Presbyterians. Ann also introduced me to the rabbi whose synagogue was across the street from Saint Margaret's.

One of the highlights of my involvement in the Christian Living Room dialogue was that, with the cooperation of young Episcopalian minister, we organized a pulpit dialogue for six evenings. A Catholic missionary priest spoke from one pulpit, while a minister from another Christian faith responded from the other pulpit. When we had finished the service, we continued the dialogue over coffee and doughnuts.

One of the positive consequences of my becoming an ecumenical priest was that I also felt more comfortable with other Christian communities in the greater Morristown area. The Methodists invited me to give four lectures at their parish on their faith's founder. The title of my series was "A Catholic priest Critiques John Wesley." The congregation seemed to enjoy the series, and the church was full every Sunday evening.

While serving as associate pastor at St. Margaret's, I also became familiar with the Stewardship program practiced in the High Episcopal church in Morristown. While the Catholic parishes focused on weekly money donations collected by the ushers, the Episcopal Church appealed to the congregation to share not only their "Treasure" but also their "Time" and "Talent" with their church.

Under the heading of "Treasure," the ministers asked the laity to donate a percentage of their income in the weekly collections. They invited some members to donate their time as religious education teachers, while others volunteered to visit any of their members who were ill in hospitals, nursing homes, or their own homes. Other members of the congregation served as financial experts in administering the Church finances, while carpenters and handymen shared their talents with those who were needy in the congregation or in the community, whether High Episcopal members or not.

In May 1969 I received a master's degree in pastoral counseling. Soon after, the director of the diocesan Family Life Bureau, Father John Derricks, requested that Bishop Casey appoint me as his assistant director.

Father Derricks was already dealing with the challenge of his duties as pastor at the large Assumption of the Blessed Virgin Mary Parish. In his separate duties as bureau director, Father Derricks clearly needed help with implementing bureau programs in the 80 parishes in the diocese. He perhaps felt that, with my new degree, I was much better qualified than he to develop counseling programs for engaged couples, couples with marital difficulties and dysfunctional families.

Looking back now, I realize that the groundwork for my transition to successful pastor at St. Vincent's was taking strong shape.

CHAPTER 4

Getting Ready to Heal Saint Vincent's

I called Father Joe at Saint Vincent's. I felt comfortable doing this because I knew him both personally and professionally. As soon as he heard my voice he congratulated me and welcomed me to Madison as his new boss. When I asked, "How are things at Saint Vincent's?"

His voice changed, and he asked me defensively, "What do you mean by that?" I then asked him, "Why did your boss request a transfer?"

"Are you serious? We never talk about things like that at the dinner table. All I know was that he didn't want the one that everybody expected to replace him." "You mean Steve Patch?" I said. "Yes" was Joe's answer.

I changed the subject, "Joe, I am happy to know that you are going to be on my team. I remember you were first a student with the Salesian Community and decided not to be ordained a Salesian, but chose to be ordained, like me, for the Diocese of Paterson."

"You have a good memory." he replied. "I am guessing, Joe, that you know as much about Liturgy as I do about Psychology. The Salesians are very good liturgists." He replied in a tone that could be interpreted either as humor or sarcasm. "Thank you, Doctor Corr."

"Joe, I want to meet with Father Ed and yourself, sometime before I go up Madison to take over on June 1. I also want you two to be present on June 1 when I meet with Monsignor as he transfers the leadership of the parish to me. "Joe seemed surprised, so I added, "When I meet with you and Ed next week, I will explain how I plan to share the leadership of the parish with both of you. It is going to be very different than what you are now used to under Monsignor."

I treated the two of them to lunch the following week. That was the first time I met Ed. He had an interesting background. He had finished his studies before his ordination at the American Theological Seminary in Rome. He was not aware of my background, that I had a Masters in Pastoral Counseling and a doctorate in Family Life Education from Columbia University, New York. I was told later, by one of his friends, that he was surprised that I was not a typical Irish priest, who played a lot of golf and enjoyed going to the racetrack to bet on the horses.

During the meeting I explained, how I believed a pastoral team would administer a parish, versus the traditional style of the "head-honcho" pastor serving alone as the only decision maker for the parish community. I suggested we could meet on Monday mornings about 9:30 AM, unless we had a funeral at that time. We would read the scriptures for the following Sunday mass, and share with each other what should be the subject for our homilies for the mass we would be celebrating.

I confess now that I had an ulterior motive. Since I was forty-four years old and trained in the seminary during the Pre-Vatican Council II era, and they were ten or fifteen years younger than I and had experienced their training in the Post-Vatican II era, I could learn their approach to preaching on the scriptures. In return I could share with them my expertise as a pre-marriage educator.

The next topic in our meeting was more challenging. I told them that if we agreed to administer the parish as a pastoral team then I needed to share all administrative decisions with them. Examples would be hiring new staff, organizing parish fundraisers and something as incidental as distributing the parish bulletin before mass or after mass.

Each of us has one vote and if we add new members to the pastoral team then they would have a vote and the majority would decide. Since I was by Canon Law legally responsible for all administrative decisions I had retain the power of veto, that I would, only use in an emergency.

Father Ed surprised me when he asked, "How can we trust you, that you are telling us the truth?" I just kept quiet and looked over at Joe. Joe turned toward Ed and said quietly but with some passion,

"Ed, you don't have to worry about Finbarr, I am familiar with all he has done for families in the diocese over the past ten years. He was appointed a therapist for priests and nuns by Bishop Rodimer. I was one of his clients, off and on, for a couple of years, and have one hundred percent trust in him."

Father Ed said, "I am tired of being treated as a young boy. I trust you, Joe, and I believe I can trust you too, Finbarr. I have studied the Documents of Vatican Council II and believe you, Finbarr, are attempting to change St. Vincent's into a Post Vatican II parish by creating a Pastoral Team. You can count on me to be there when Monsignor hands over the parish to you on June 1."

I went back to the Family Life Office, which was

also my residence, on 17th Avenue in Paterson. I packed my books in the trunk of my car. Two days later, on May 28, I drove to 26 Green Village Rd. in Madison. I arrived at the rectory a half hour later than the time the Monsignor had expected me. He was not happy when he took me upstairs to his office on the second floor. I switched to my therapeutic mode to avoid being sucked into a meaningless squabble.

I said, "The traffic on Route 46 was 'stop and go' all the way from Clifton to Morristown. I am sorry if I screwed up your schedule. Will you please call Fathers Edward and Joe to come to this meeting."

"Why?" he yelled.

"Because I want them to participate with me in the administration of Saint Vincent Martyr Parish."

He replied with a sarcastic tone, "Huh, you are one of those kind of leaders?" To which I replied, "I didn't change the Church, the Fathers at the Second Vatican Council did. We hope to create a Post Vatican II parish here in Madison."

A while later the two associate pastors walked in and took seats. I opened my notebook and used my agenda to run a brief meeting.

Looking towards Monsignor, I said, "I wish you good luck in your new assignment. By the way, I didn't ask to be transferred here, Bishop Rodimer sent me." (Msgr. ignored my comment)

Addressing Joe and Ed, "I have invited you both to join me in creating a Vatican II parish community and I am grateful that you both have accepted."

Monsignor looked distracted and said, "Can we get on with the meeting? I am already a half hour late for my next appointment." So I chose a topic that I knew would engage Monsignor "How is the financial situation here at Saint Vincent's?"

"Not good, if you can get the Gu***eas to give more than two bucks a Sunday, you are a better man than me." I cringed at that moment, beginning to understand why the Bishop wanted to send me to Saint Vincent's.

The meeting continued with Fathers Joe and Ed sharing with me the number of organizations in the parish and how we needed to create a closer relationship with Saint Vincent's School, which is located 20 yards from the rectory. Father Ed added "The enrollment is dropping."

Monsignor started looking at his watch and I sensed that he wanted to leave the meeting, so I asked one more question that surprised him. "I know you are required by Canon Law to have two lay trustees. May I ask if they participate at all in the financial management of the parish?"

He replied in a muffled voice, "Not at all, they are two old men, they just sign the financial report annually. I suggest that you get two younger parishioners, if you want them to participate in the financial administration of the parish." He waved to the three of us and left his office.

Joe and Ed smiled, took me downstairs and introduced me to Phyllis Giannone, the parish secretary. She was a warm and friendly woman, and I looked forward to working with her.

CHAPTER 5

The First Month as Pastor of Saint Vincent's

On June 1, 1979, I was sad leaving 476 17th Ave, Paterson, NJ which had served as my residence and office for ten years. This is where the Family Life movement began as a full-time agency of the Diocese of Paterson. It was created and grew to have an impact on the sixty-five parishes in Sussex, Morris and Passaic counties. It was the only agency in the Diocese that had an ecumenical board, called the Family Life Board of Governors. They assisted me, the Director, in raising money and with publicity and helped in co-sponsoring Family Day rallies in both Clifton Stadium and Rutgers Stadium.

I was full of hope as I drove west on Route 46 toward Madison and I remembered Bishop Rodimer's words on that Monday morning, after I objected to his invitation to become pastor of Saint Vincent Martyr parish.

"I believe you are exactly what the Parish needs right now." I was determined not to let our bishop down.

I had packed my bags, put my golf clubs in the trunk and to the surprise of the staff at the Family Life Office, I decided to take my beloved Irish (born) setter, Rory, along with me.

FR Finbarr Corr at home in New Jersey with his Red Setter dog, bred by Dan Shanaghy (circa. 1974)

Rory and I arrived at 26 Green Village Road on Friday June 1, 2:00 PM. Msgr had left for his assignment in the inner-city of Paterson.

Larry, the Parish janitor, helped me move my books, clothing and personal items to my new office and an attached bedroom on the second floor.

Father Joe welcomed me and assisted me arranging my books on the shelves in my office. Father Ed was visiting the sick parishioners at Morristown Memorial Hospital, three miles away. Larry, who loved dogs, agreed to take care of Rory and feed him while I organized my life as pastor of Saint Vincent's.

Phyllis, our parish secretary, embraced me and told me her husband Anthony was excited to welcome the first Irish-born pastor to the parish. I learned later that since he retired he had helped Larry by cleaning the Church every week.

Father Joe said over dinner that he and Ed would discuss with me how I wanted to be introduced at the five masses on Saturday evening and Sunday morning.

Having had to fix all my meals, living alone on 17th Avenue, I excitedly waited to have my first meal served by Theresa the cook, who had the reputation of being the best rectory cook in the diocese.

At 3:00 PM I went out to the church parking lot to meet the children, who were waiting for their parents to pick them up after school. I put Rory on a leash and took him with me. Since he was not accustomed to children in the Family Life office, he didn't allow them to come over and pat him on the head.

Sister Alicia, the school principal, knew me as the agent from the Diocese who had introduced Education in Human Sexuality (Sex Ed) to all the Catholic grammar and high schools of the Diocese. She, too, gave me a warm welcome and humorously asked, "What did we do to deserve getting a sexpert as our new pastor?"

The three of us padres had a delicious dinner, served promptly at 6:00 PM by the not-so-charming but wonderful cook, Theresa. She welcomed me to the parish without reaching out to shake my hand.

While she was back in the kitchen, Father Joe whispered to me, "Theresa likes to decide what to serve us at each meal. You will discover, as times goes on, she doesn't serve the same dinner twice in two weeks. Wait until you see the dinner she serves when the bishop comes here to administer Confirmation to the children."

I just smiled back at Joe and said, "That is one issue that we, the pastoral team, won't have to worry about during our weekly meetings."

Father Joe initiated the discussion on who I would be introduced to my new spiritual family on Saturday evening and at the Sunday morning masses. He said, "Finbarr, I feel you should be celebrant at the 5:00 PM mass on Saturday evening and the 10:30 AM on Sunday. If you wish, I will give you a brief welcome from the pulpit before you begin."

Father Ed entered the discussion and said, "Since I am scheduled to say the 7 PM on Saturday and the 12 Noon on Sunday I would prefer to introduce you at the end of both masses."

"In that case Ed, I will give a very brief thank you to the parishioners, who gave me a warm welcome."

Joe smiled, coming up with a different proposal, saying, "Since you are saying two masses and preaching at both, do you mind preaching at my mass at 9:00 AM? I will introduce you after I read the gospel. I had no choice but to answer, "If you wish, Joe," I replied.

Using a little Irish humor, I got a positive response to my homily at the 5:00 PM mass on Saturday. Celebrating the 10:30 AM mass on Sunday was a bigger challenge, as it included the four-part harmony choir directed by Vicky Martell, an experienced director of civic concerts in cities outside New Jersey.

During my homily I listed Pope John XXIII as my favorite pope and ended up saying I hope Pope John, who is now in heaven, will rejoice at the family oriented parish that Fathers Ed, Joe and I plan to create in conjunction with next year's *Year of the Family* in 1980. To my surprise an applause that initiated with the choir spread throughout the congregation. I replied, "Thank you very much."

There was only one incident that happened over that first weekend that could be interpreted either as a challenge to me or a criticism of my predecessor. An older gentleman, who I found out later was of Italian descent, approached me in the vestibule as I greeted parishioners following the 5:00 PM liturgy. He waited to be the last one to greet me.

"Welcome to Saint Vincent's Father Corr. "If I donate $5,000 to the church, would you put the altar back where it belongs?"

"I will accept your donation on one condition - that the first meeting to organize the transfer of the altar back to where it was, will happen the week after I am transferred to another parish."

I never received the donation.

CHAPTER 6

Creating a Pastoral Team

The three of us who were members of the Pastoral Team - Joe, Ed and I - met as we agreed in the rectory conference room at 9:30 AM on Monday morning.

I shared with them that I had learned a lot about leadership from the Family Life Board of Governors during the past six years. I accepted their compliments after I told them how I had successfully introduced "Sex Ed" to 90% of the Catholic grammar and high schools of the Diocese. Likewise, I accepted their criticism when they told me that the Family Life staff and myself hadn't done a good job of advertising our programs in the public press and Catholic press.

Joe asked a very significant question, "Do you plan to incorporate lay leaders of St. Vincent's in the administration of the parish?"

"Absolutely," I assured them.

"That is going to be very different than what we and the parishioners are accustomed to," replied Ed.

I replied "As you know, Ed, the cardinals, bishops and theologians who participated in Vatican Council II under the leadership of my favorite Pope (John XXIII) left us a very different Church. The baptized laity are now the 'People of God' and are expected to participate with the hierarchy in evangelizing the world."

Joe smiled and asked, "Do we have to make all these changes overnight?"

"Not really, Joe." "We have to get our own act together as a team before we involve the laity. I am thinking of asking help from someone you already know. That person is Father Kenneth Lasch, the assistant chancellor of the Diocese who, together with Sister Marie Schultejann, provides this service to parishes."

Ed changed the topic, "If you are looking for two trustees to replace the older gentlemen who served with Monsignor, I have the names of two candidates that you can invite to serve."

Joe asked, "Who are they?"

"You know them, Joe. I am thinking of Dick Annese, who is active as vice president at Chubb Insurance and Frank Weller, who lives on Green Avenue is an investor on Wall Street."

Joe smiled and said, "Leave it to you, Ed."

I suggested, "Since you both know them, and I don't, with your permission I'll call them and invite them to fill the positions of the two retiring trustees." They agreed.

Since we all were communicating well, I thought I should share Bishop Rodimer's reason for asking me to become pastor of St. Vincent's Parish. I began by asking them, "What has been happening to the parish in the last few years?"

There was no answer. I then asked, "Why did that elderly parishioner offer me several thousand dollars if I brought back the main altar to the sanctuary?"

Joe responded, "I wasn't here when Monsignor restructured the interior of the church. He replaced the traditional main altar with the new round marble altar that is now the center of the church and placed the pews without kneelers all around it."

I asked, "What was wrong with that? I liked offering mass there yesterday. I felt like the whole family of the parish was gathered around me in prayer."

Ed jumped in and said, "The problem was not how the renovation turned out. Many of the parishioners felt that they were not consulted about the changes. About one hundred families left the parish. The older gentleman who spoke to you on Saturday after the 5:30 PM mass was typical of those parishioners who were angry at Monsignor for making all those changes in 'their' church without 'their permission.'"

I replied, "Our job as a pastoral team is to heal the community and invite all of the parishioners, young and old, to become active participants in a post-Vatican Council community of faith. We won't campaign to bring back the parishioners who left us and went to another parish, but, if they return, we will welcome them home."

I also introduced the concept of Stewardship as a theological belief that one God created the universe and all that it is in it and that Christians have a responsibility to take care of what God created. I explained, "Religiously, Stewardship involves individuals sharing their Time, Talent and Treasure to the service of God. When we introduce Stewardship into St. Vincent's parish, we as the pastoral team will invite people to share in ministering to the eighteen hundred families of our parish."

I continued, "Many lay people, especially those with teaching experience, are ideal volunteers to teach religion to the public-school students and help prepare them to receive the sacraments of Holy Communion and Confirmation. When it comes to sharing their treasure, we will be using the word 'Tithe' requesting individuals and families to donate a specific percentage of their income to enable the priests and staff to meet the needs of all the families in the parish."

We concluded the first meeting of the Pastoral Team with Joe reading the three passages scheduled for the following Sunday's mass: a reading from the Book of the Prophet Isaiah, the second reading from the First Letter of Saint Paul to the Corinthians, and the third from the Gospel of Saint Mark.

Ed then shared his thoughts about how we could use Jesus' message "Be watchful, be alert, you do not know when the time will come" from Mark's gospel in our homilies that Sunday. He said, "Jesus does not tell us when we are going to pass from this life to the next. He wants us to watch, pray and keep awake. This is the key to living a virtuous life. That is why Jesus makes the end of life for all of us uncertain." I left the meeting with a sense of unity of purpose and was optimistic that the three of us could work together quite well.

More help soon appeared. Because I had already

been visiting a YMCA for a few years to renew my physical fitness, I decided to join the Madison YMCA, which was only a half-mile away from the rectory. There I was fortunate to renew my friendship with several old friends who were very happy to see me back in the area.

Two of them who were devout Catholics - Matt Sitter from Convent Station and Carl Vitolo, a parishioner of St. Vincent's Parish - offered to help me initiate the concept of team ministry. Both were experienced businessmen and had followed the Vatican II changes. Matt shared his salesman's experience with me and gave me insights on how to introduce a new style of ministry to the parishioners. I shared that I was planning to introduce Stewardship into the parish. Offering more help, Carl enthusiastically said, "Finbarr, I have a longtime business connection with an Episcopalian priest who lives and works in New York City. He has successfully introduced Stewardship to his congregation and I know he would be only too happy to come out to Madison and help you initiate it at St. Vincent's."

My fear of whether the Italian parishioners of St. Vincent's would accept a pastor with an Irish brogue had disappeared. I now felt buoyed by an "all-hands-on-deck" sense of team and looked forward to my new life adventure as pastor of St. Vincent's.

CHAPTER 7

Adding Trustees and Lay Advisors

M att Sitter and Carl Vitolo offered to meet me in the rectory to share their experience as successful business men and show me how our pastoral team should approach our goal of creating a post-Vatican II parish. I shared with them, confidentially, why I thought Bishop Rodimer asked me to give up my job of director of the Family Life Bureau to become a healing pastor in Saint Vincent's. Since Carl was an active parishioner for several years and Italian by heritage, he had a better understanding than Matt or me as to why I was called upon by the bishop to become the pastor of Saint Vincent's.

Looking at me, Carl said, "Finbarr, you are the first Irish-born pastor appointed here by the bishop. Your predecessor was born in the parish and, like me, is of Italian descent. The bishop should not have appointed him to succeed his predecessor, who was of Irish heritage and didn't have good pastoral skills. On the other hand, you have the reputation of being a successful leader of the Family Life Bureau. Our diocesan newspaper, the Beacon, reported on your success in organizing over 1,000 volunteers in launching the Family Day rally at Rutgers Stadium. Other people have told me that you are a very successful marriage and family therapist. Your goal of creating a Post-Vatican II parish here in Madison is not going to be easy. You are the first pastor, to my knowledge, who has asked lay business men like Matt and I to help you. And we are happy to help you, Fathers Ed and Joe reach your goal."

Matt added, "My wife Marlene and I attend Saint Thomas Moore Church in Convent Station. We were told that almost one hundred families switched from Saint Vincent's Parish to ours because of how the pastor, without consulting them, ripped the whole church apart, removed the beautiful main altar that one of these families had donated and filled the church with new pews that had no kneelers."

Not wanting to spend the whole evening criticizing my predecessor, I asked them, "Let's move on. How can you help us?"

Matt asked, "Are your two associates, Father Ed and Father Joe, buying into your concept of creating a family-oriented parish?"

"I believe they are going to be as enthusiastic as I am. I feel Father Ed is particularly happy that all three of us will share authority. He told me at one of our team meetings we have every Monday morning that he is tired of being treated as a young boy all the time (my predecessor called him Eddie). He was educated at the Gregorian Theological Seminary in Rome, while the Vatican Council was in progress (1962-65). He graduated with a master's degree in theology and, being familiar with the theological discussions the Fathers of Vatican Council II shared with Pope John XXIII, I believe he can share even more insights into what a Post Vatican II parish will look like than either Joe or I, who were not in Rome during the Second Vatican Council."

Carl complimented me on our choice of trustees, Dick Annese and Frank Weller. I corrected him saying, "You should complement Father Ed when you see him, because he is the one who nominated them."

I shared with Carl and Matt what I thought the job descriptions of the new trustees should be, i.e. recording the weekly parish income and monthly expenses. I emphasized that I didn't want to spend my time worrying about the finances of the parish.

I planned to meet with them monthly, receive their comments on parish income and ask them for input regarding the feasibility of hiring additional staff, such as a youth minister, to help the Pastoral Team. Both Matt and Carl agreed and advised me to listen to their advice. Matt added, "You should not run the parish with a financial deficit."

The rest of the meeting focused on how to introduce Stewardship into the parish. Matt said he had never been in a parish where the priests introduced this program. Carl said, "I am not surprised, Matt. My understanding is that it began in non-Catholic Christian churches. It is based on scripture and focuses on relationship building within the community of the church and doing what Finbarr, Ed and Joe are planning to do to create a family atmosphere in the parish."

"Well done, Carl" I replied. "The parish doesn't belong to the priests, although some priests act as if it is their parish. The parish belongs to the people and we are here to serve the people and help create a community."

In preparation for introducing Stewardship into the parish, I did some research in the scriptures and found a passage in The Epistle of Saint Paul to the Colossians that was insightful.

"He is the image of the invisible God, the first born of every creature. For in him were created all things in the heavens and on the earth, things visible and things invisible, whether Thrones or Dominations, or Principalities or Powers. All things have been created through and unto him." (Colossians 1: 16.)

As reported in the Gospel of Saint Luke, Jesus talked about stewardship. He used parables about handling money to teach deeper principles about discipleship and reminded us that our hearts follow our treasure: "Do not be afraid little flock, for it has pleased the Father to give you the kingdom. Sell what you have and give alms. Make for yourselves purses that do not grow old, a treasure in heaven, where neither thief draws near, or moths destroys. For where your treasure is, there also will you heart be." (The Gospel of St. Luke 12:32-34)

The meeting with my two friends Matt and Carl gave me a lot of confidence that Fathers Ed, Joe and myself would be able to create a post-Vatican II parish.

I chose a restaurant convenient to Frank Weller's home for my first luncheon meeting with my prospective trustees Frank and Dick Annese. I didn't want to impose too much on Frank, knowing that he needed to be near his home to communicate with

Wall Street during their business hours.

Trustee Frank Weller

The first thing that Dick and Frank did was to congratulate me on my appointment as pastor of their parish. I decided not to tell them why I thought the bishop had requested that I give up my position of leading the Family Life movement to take on this challenging assignment. I didn't know much about their background, except what Father Ed had announced at the team meeting. If they were friends or admirers of my predecessor, they would not be impressed if I told them that the bishop sent me as healer to a dysfunctional parish. I chose to introduce myself to them.

"I don't know if you know my background. Besides being an Irish-born priest, who continued his education after coming from Ireland in August 1960, I received a master's degree in Pastoral Counseling at Iona College and a doctorate in Family Life Education at Columbia University. According to Carl Vitolo, who has volunteered to help Fathers Ed, Joe and I introduce Stewardship in the parish, all of you know of my success of using 1,000 volunteers to sponsor a successful a statewide Family Day rally at Rutgers Stadium."

They both smiled, and Frank added, "You got a big write-up in the Beacon last fall."

I smiled back and said, "I learned a lot this past six years, working with an ecumenical board of governors in the Diocese. I have shared with Ed and Joe that I would like to continue this approach as the three of us form a pastoral team and facilitate creating a family oriented post- Vatican II parish."

I paused for a moment and asked them, "Are you familiar with how Pope John XXIII changed the Catholic church to define the Church as the 'People of God'? In other words, the Church is no longer just the hierarchy, but all baptized Catholics are the People of God."

I looked them in the eyes and said, "If you accept my invitation to become the new Trustees you will share the financial administration of the parish with us three priests."

They both smiled, and Dick said, "Speaking personally, I feel it is an honor to be invited into what I believe is a going to be a total parish renewal. I don't know if Father Ed told you, my dear wife died recently, we had no children and my volunteering will help fill in the empty feeling I have each evening when I come home from work."

"Thank you, Dick, I do appreciate your donating your time and your talent as a financial expert. Your input will be very valuable when we introduce the third phase of Stewardship in a few months, inviting parishioners to donate a percentage of their income to the parish."

Frank added, "I feel very privileged to be invited to join Dick in this worthy cause. Father Ed is a good friend of my wife Fran and I and he is very excited about having you take over as pastor and inviting him and Joe to be part of the pastoral team. I can't wait to call him and tell him I appreciate him nominating me to be a trustee with Dick. Thank you, Father Finbarr, for accepting the invitation to become our pastor."

CHAPTER 8

Changing of the Guard

As part of laying the ground work to move forward, we decided to put closure on the activities of my predecessor. As reported earlier, our pastoral team decided to replace the two aging, inactive trustees with two younger men who would be active on a weekly basis in the financial management of the parish. Fortunately, one of the older gentlemen decided to leave Madison and move to a retirement village. Our pastoral team honored the other, Mr. Toto, a retired contractor-by presenting him with a retirement plaque at the 10:30 AM mass on Sunday.

Since we hadn't announced publicly that both Dick Annese and Frank Weller had agreed to be the new trustees, a rich, self-made man came to me after the mass we honored Mr. Toto and offered, "Father Corr, if you wish, I will help you find two trustees. I am available myself if you want me."

I replied politely. "Thank you, Sir. Our pastoral team has already accepted Mr. Annese and Mr. Weller as our replacement trustees."

The man became very angry, saying, "If that is how you plan to run Saint Vincent's, I am leaving the parish and taking my annual $6,000 Christmas donation with me."

"I am sorry, Sir" I replied, "if you don't understand what is involved in creating a post-Vatican II, family-oriented parish. I hope you and your family are not disappointed with your decision."

Fathers Ed and Joe were not surprised when I shared the story with them.

Father Ed added, "We are better off without him. He tries to control everybody with his money".

Now we were ready to start organizing the first cultural celebration of Family Year 1980. Ten parishioners joined our planning committee. I invited Gloria Agel, who I met through her vivacious daughter Angela, a fourth-grader in our grammar school. I also invited Fran Mantone, who had good organizational skills. Gerry Gannon, who had volunteered earlier to help organize Family Year 1980 now became active in organizing the first cultural event i.e. Italian night.

I welcomed everybody to the meeting and thanked them for attending. They could tell by my presentation that the celebration of Italian night was going to be an enjoyable affair. I said, "Father Ed and Father Joe, a New-York born Italian, are as enthusiastic about Italian night as I will be when we celebrate my Irish culture on Saint Patricks' Day in mid-March. I may even dance a jig on that night!"

Father Joe said, "Father Finbarr has much more experience in organizing Family Day rallies on diocesan and state level, so we will rely on his experience in celebrating our Italian culture socially, liturgically and artistically, as we end the celebration with a banquet featuring the best Italian cuisine and wine."

"You are correct, Joe" I replied. "If I was still director of the Family Life Bureau, celebrating Family Year 1980 would be a diocesan program. But since we are in Madison, we can still use the "Celebrate Family" program created by the United States Conference of Catholic Bishops to motivate the whole parish to become a family."

I said to Joe, "Tell the committee what liturgical celebration you proposed to Ed and me for the Italian weekend."

"I plan to recruit an Italian priest to say mass in Italian on Saturday evening before the banquet. I will ask him to tell the congregation in his homily how Italians have contributed to the growth of Catholicism over the centuries. I also plan to ask Vicky Martell to have the choir sings hymns in both Latin and Italian.

Gerry Gannon raised the question, "Has the pastoral team decided when this celebration will take place? I would suggest that we hold it in mid-February, close to Valentine's Day." Over half the committee nodded their heads. I asked, "Do any of you object to celebrating it in February just after Valentine's Day?" Nobody objected.

Father Ed said, "Since I volunteered to gather Italian art and paintings to set it up the art show in the hallway, on the way into the school, I will be asking a few of you to help me. If you know of any parishioners who have pieces of Italian art in their home, please let me know and I will call them. I have a few contacts in New York, and I plan to ask them if they would loan me some small pieces of Italian art and pictures for display at the party."

The meeting ended on a high note at 9:00 PM with a commitment to meet bi-weekly until Valentine's Day.

CHAPTER 9

The Year of the Family

Saint Paul in his Epistle to the Romans tells us how Christians should behave and what are their primary duties in life,

> "I exhort you therefore, brethren, by the mercy of God, to present your bodies as a sacrifice, living holy, pleasing to God--- your spiritual service. And do not be conformed to the world, but be transformed in the newness of your mind, that you may discern what is the good and acceptable and perfect will of God."

(Romans: 12:1-2)

I used this quote to motivate my colleagues Ed and Joe to begin planning the Year of the Family.

Ed said, "This is going to be easy, as we celebrate the different cultures in the town of Madison. Obviously, we must begin celebrating the Italian

Family, since most of our parishioners were either born in Italy or are of Italian descent."

"Tanti Auguri, Eduardo. "(Congratulations Edward.) I responded.

Joe said, "I will organize an Italian liturgy, to be celebrated by an Italian born priest."

"Since I love Italian food," I said, "I will ask Gloria Agel and Fran Mantone to have several of their Italian friends join them in organizing a four course Italian dinner."

"Wow, Wow" yelled Joe. "You are going all out." "Yes, Joe, if we organize this correctly, we can add one hundred parishioners of Italian descent to donate their Time and Treasure as part of their Stewardship.

Some of them would join the Confraternity of Christian Doctrine (C.C.D.) teaching public school students about Jesus, the sacraments etc. We also need to expand our youth ministry. The records show that less than 40 % of the students who attend Madison public high school attend religious instruction and participate in Catholic Youth Organization (C.Y.O.) activity. When we increase our Sunday collections I will discuss with our trustees hiring a full-time youth minister."

Ed made another contribution, "Celebrating the Italian culture should include Italian art and music. Since I visited many homes, owned by Italians over the years, who have demonstrated a love of Italian culture, we can borrow their art and set up a display in the school auditorium, during the weekend when we have the Italian liturgy and enjoying Fran Mantone's and Gloria Agel's delicious Italian cuisine."

To initiate the promotion of THE YEAR OF THE FAMILY I included the following scriptural passage in my regular weekly column in the parish bulletin.

> "Holy Father keep in thy name those whom you have given me, that they may be one even as we are. While I was with them I kept them in thy name. Those whom you gave me I guarded; and not one of them perished except the son of perdition, in order that the scripture might be fulfilled. But now I am coming to thee; and these I speak in the world, in order that they may have my joy made full in themselves."
>
> (John: 17:11-13)

"Our pastoral team, Father Ed, Father Joe and I cordially invite you to volunteer to serve on the _Year of the Family_ committee, so that we may have input from all the different cultures that make up Saint Vincent's Parish. I am asking you to guess which culture we will celebrate first. I can tell you it won't be mine i.e. Irish!"

That Sunday afternoon the phone rang in the rectory. As I picked up the receiver, a friendly voice introduced himself to me, "Hi Father Finbarr, I am Gerry Gannon from Florham Park. My wife Mary and I switched parishes, as we were impressed with your bio published in the diocesan newspaper. I am a resigned Catholic priest, just one of five such priests who are active in the parish."

"Thank you, Gerry, for the phone call; I am guessing that you are responding to my article in today's bulletin."

"That's right Father."

I quickly replied, "Gerry, since you are still an ordained priest, you may call me just Finbarr. What is your career right now?"

"I am a registered social worker and would be happy to help you, Fathers Joe and Ed organize the Year of the Family," he replied, adding "I agree with you, we should not celebrate our Irish culture first; we can do that in March and wear our shamrocks as we dance an Irish jig."

Gerry was the first of several parishioners to call the rectory and volunteer to help us organize The Year of the Family.

As part of the Family Year celebration in 1981, the heritage of our Polish parishioners was highlighted on Saturday, January 31, at 7 PM. Events began with a polka mass. Father John Podgorny, pastor of Holy Rosary Parish Passaic, was the invited celebrant, with Father Ed, Joe and I as concelebrants. In his homily Father John reflected on Poland's contribution to the Catholic Church. A statue of our Lady of Czestochowa was carried in as the mass began.

St. Vincent parishioner Kathy Pratola spoke from the pulpit on how the Polish experience in the US began in 1608 when the ship Mary and Margaret docked in Jamestown, Virginia. Many passengers from other European countries were escaping from political, social and economic persecution, but not the first Poles. They came for the adventure.

Kathy reported that the influx in 1830 brought middle and upper class Polish who were fleeing

Russian rule. The massive peasant emigration of Poles in 1855 and 1856 reportedly made up 14.6 % of the total immigration in those years.

The ensuing celebration in the school auditorium featured Polish cuisine and lively music by the Dick Pillar Polka Band. Ed avoided dancing the Polka, but Joe and I gave it a shot. Kathy Pratola was shocked when I practically swept her off her feet by swinging her around during my interpretation of the polka.

We invited Bishop Rodimer to be the principal celebrant of the mass for the Diamond Jubilee of the Parish on June 27, 1981. We three members of the pastoral team concelebrated. Priests and nuns who had served in the parish during the previous 75 years were invited to participate.

The response was very positive according to Fran Mantone, who coordinated the invitations. Jim Penders and Marty Stockert organized the Jubilee journal with helpful input from Father Ed and 12 other parishioners. The journal contained several pages of pictures recording historical events during the previous 75 years. As usual, a social followed in the school auditorium.

During the celebration, we posthumously honored the three Corbett sisters - Helen, Lucille and

Adele - as residents of the first permanent Church of St. Vincent's at 69 Ridge Avenue in Madison. We also honored deceased parishioner John Corbett, the builder of the newer brick, stone and mortar St. Vincent's church structure on Green Village Road.

History records that the St. Vincent Martyr church property was purchased in 1903 from Peter and Ellen Condon. In 1891 they purchased it from Elizabeth Bennett, who inherited it from General Edward E. Potter, a Union Army officer during the American Civil War.

I found myself wondering, if the Corbett sisters could return to St. Vincent's Parish, would they admire the spirit of family community that we, the pastoral team, had created?

While the program to organize the Year of the Family looked promising, I was anxious to know what if anything I could do to stimulate the youth ministry program. Fr. Joe tried to reassure me that because of the Catholic Youth Organization (CYO) there was plenty of activity for the teenagers of the parish. With the help of adult lay advisors, the CYO organized a basketball league with teams from different parishes competing. The teenagers had dances and bus trips to the New Jersey shore.

Addressing Fr. Joe, I said, "While all this social activity is impressive, what is the parish doing on a regular basis to assist the teenagers, who attend Madison High School, to grow in their faith and become active adult Catholics? Joe there is something missing, if only thirty teenagers come to religious instructions weekly. My guess is that because our parish boasts of having eighteen hundred families, there has to be about three hundred Catholic teenagers who attend Madison High and only thirty of them attend Catholic instructions on Sunday evenings." Joe replied, "I cannot argue with you. I see where you are coming from. Maybe it is time for us to hire a full-time youth minister to organize these religious instructions."

"Joe, I am ready, but the two Trustees are not. We have agreed not to get into deficit spending. When we get the Stewardship program going, I expect a big increase in our regular Sunday collections and then we can go ahead and hire a full-time youth minister."

While waiting for that moment, I decided to conduct an experiment myself. I called one of the adult advisors for the Sunday evening high school program and told him I was going to give a three-week workshop for the teenagers on a provocative subject, entitled "Teenagers and Their Sexuality." The program was held in a small room in the basement of the school with seating for forty students. Thirty-one students and two adult advisors turned up for first session.

Having taught psychology for a few years, I knew that it was important to get the teenagers attention in first three or four minutes or you might lose them for the total hour. To help them get used to having me as their teacher, I came into the classroom about ten minutes before the class was due to begin at 7:00 PM. I had each of them introduce themselves casually to me.

At 7:05 PM I walked to the blackboard and wrote in large letters "SEX"!! and asked, casually, "What do you know about this?" There was a trickle of snickers throughout the room and one of the brash young gentleman decided he was going to challenge the new pastor with "What do you know about sex? You are a priest." I was ready for him.

"Stand up, Michael."

When he did, I sat down in his seat and said, "You seem to know more than me. Why don't you lead the discussion this evening?" The thirty students applauded, realizing that I had called Michael's bluff and was beating him at his own game.

While Michael was embarrassed, he said "Ok, Father you win."

I didn't want to embarrass him any further and have his peers gang up on him, so I continued with, "Michael is partly right. None of us, especially me, know everything about the beautiful gift of human sexuality that God has given to us. We don't understand the drive in each of us that craves intimacy with the opposite sex." There was absolute silence in the room. I believe I captured their attention with the vulnerable statement, "none of us, especially me." If I had foolishly said "Listen to me, I have a doctorate in Family Life Education from Columbia University" they would have turned me off, as quickly as you could say Jack Robinson. I continued, "We men are strange animals. We are attracted to girls and we want more than an emotional relationship with these beautiful creatures. If they would cooperate, we would want a physical union."

Michael's eyes were ready to pop out of his head, as he never heard a priest speaking so openly about sex before.

CHAPTER 10

Teenagers and Their Sexuality

I decided to leave Michael alone and move on to discussing female sexuality with the few young ladies in the class. I posed the question "Why are women so attracted to us men, craving our attention? Our romantic gestures? Wanting to be in our presence and demanding security?" The ten or twelve teenage girls loved it, giggled, and wanted to get involved in the discussion.

A tall blond named Dorothy stood up and said, "Father we expected you to lecture us on how it is a mortal sin to have sex with a guy before we get married and how dangerous it is being involved in passionate kissing and allowing guys to touch our bare breasts."

"I know that you already know these facts, Dorothy. But has anybody ever talked to you before we began these discussions about our heavenly Father's gift to all of us . . . about His gift of human sexuality to the whole human race?"

"You are right, Father" Dorothy replied. "You are the first priest I know of who has shared the positive gift from God of human sexuality to all of us."

I replied, "And this is coming from one who has dedicated himself to celibacy for the rest of his life."

Before I concluded the session at 8 PM, I asked them a simple question. "Did you enjoy our discussion here this evening?"

There was a positive response from the whole group. One of the two adult advisors stood up and said. "This evening was just a beginning. Father Corr will be here for the next two Sunday evenings. Thank you, Father." Addressing the whole body of students, he added, "We want you to go back to the high school tomorrow and invite all your Catholic friends to join you next week. What you experienced this evening is just a beginning. Father Corr, Father Ed and Father Joe are in the process of changing our parish into a spiritual family. As one of the volunteers for youth ministry in St. Vincent's, I am very pleased to be part of this renewal of our parish. I cannot wait to see all the activity that the pastoral team is planning for the next few months. I look forward to seeing you and many of your friends next week."

One of the teachers at Madison High School, who had overheard two of the students talking about the session on sexuality, told the lay volunteer that one of the students said to the other, "The new pastor at St. Vincent's is an older guy, but he's cool."

I admit it felt good to be able to relate, as an almost fifty-year-old, to the teenagers in Madison. Apparently, my style of engaging the boys and girls on the first and second Sunday evenings was successful. Sixty public school students turned up on the second Sunday evening, and 100 for the final and third session.

I shared the success of my three-week experiment with Ed and Joe. They didn't seem surprised. Joe commented that my background as family therapist facilitated my approach, and he added that the sooner the trustees gave us the okay to hire a youth minister, the better our ministry to the teenagers of the parish would be.

I asked Joe, "Do you have anybody in mind for the position?"

He quickly replied, "Yes, I do. Her name is Livvy Dinneen and she lives in Chatham."

"Get me her resume and I will bring it to the Trustees when I meet them next week".

One of the parents from St. Vincent's School approached me confidentially after she heard about my successful three weeks with the teenagers. She said, "Father Corr, we have a good principal in Sister Alicia and a good faculty, but our enrollment is dropping. We need somebody with your skills to help increase enrollment."

"Thank you, Ma'am," I said. "Let me think about if for a couple of weeks."

Since I had no specific training in school administration, I didn't approach Sister Alicia directly. I started visiting the classrooms weekly, getting to know the teachers and letting the students get to know me. As a therapist I was aware that young children could easily get attached to a priest and would want to visit him at the rectory to get affirmation or a hug. As a qualified pastoral counselor who counseled families and religious, I was aware of the disorder of pedophilia. While I didn't have the malady, I didn't want parents to be suspicious. I only allowed children to visit me in my office if there were two children together; otherwise I met any single student downstairs in the presence of the parish secretaries.

Not having any children of my own, I enjoyed meeting the children in the playground. I would tease them and in turn they would tease me. One red-haired girl, Sarah, had a congenital hip problem and walked with a limp. My heart went out to her. One day after she got to know me, I gave her hug and asked, "Sarah what do you want to do when you grow up?"

She replied almost in tears, "Father Corr, I want to be a dancer." I was heartbroken and felt that I needed to give her a reply that wasn't overly pious.

"Sarah, if you have faith and trust in God, you will dance one day if it is His will. I will pray with you daily. Nothing is impossible with God." Sarah's excitement grew, and we became special friends while she was a student at St. Vincent's School. After Sarah left to enter high school, her leg improved sufficiently to allow her to walk without a limp. She and I lost contact when she and her family moved to Oregon, but I kept her in my daily prayers.

Two days before Thanksgiving in 1990 – about 10 years later when I was no longer a pastor and had married - I was shopping for a turkey in a Madison store when Maureen, a parishioner from St. Vincent's, excitedly approached me. "Finbarr, this is providential. I was looking for you. Guess who my daughter Susan is bringing to have Thanksgiving dinner with us?"

Remembering that Susan and Sarah were buddies, I exclaimed "SARAH!" I then calmly asked, "What is she up to?"

I almost fainted when Maureen said, "She has been dancing for a year with the Richmond Ballet."

"See how prayer works" I replied.

At Thanksgiving Susan drove Sarah over to our home in Convent Station to meet my wife Laurie and me. After a few pleasantries were exchanged, Sarah, still as cute as ever, said to Laurie, "Mrs. Corr, I hope you don't mind, but I love your husband." Sarah later married a guy from California. I haven't heard from her since then but am hoping that she is still dancing her heart out.

I was disappointed when Sister Alicia announced that, for personal reasons, she was leaving her job as our principal. It was also time for me to leave for a sabbatical in Rome. In my absence, Ed and Joe hired a new principal, a layman who I thought was a phony the first time I met him after my return. He would wear the same clothes to school for three or four days and would frequently take a nap with his head resting on the desk in his office. Knowing the rules about firing staff people, I sent him a letter, with a copy to the diocesan school office, warning him that his behavior was not acceptable.

Two weeks later I discovered that he was also stealing $300 per month from the school account. I sent him another warning by mail and again copied it to the Chancery Office. Three days later I invited the person who had reported the stealing to my office. I then brought the delinquent principal in to listen while the witness sat opposite him and confronted him about his immoral behavior.

I kept my cool as I said, "Sir, you are very lucky that during my six years in the seminary I learned how to control my quick Irish temper. Instead of beating you up, I am demanding that you repay our school $2,400 and leave the school within the next 45 minutes." He left the school grounds and we never heard from him again.

Our pastoral team was very lucky to hire Miss Carol Bennett, a new and dynamic principal, to replace him. From her first day on the job Miss Bennett became an active member of the school board that I had created to address curriculum issues, marketing, public relations and methods to increase enrollment. I was also fortunate that Dr. Jack Callan, a college professor and a very objective educator, agreed to head the board. To celebrate Catholic School Week, several parents spoke from the pulpit on the value of a Catholic education and explain to the congregation why we had to temporarily close eighth grade because the class enrollment didn't meet the minimum size of eight students for proper socialization.

During these few months the Pastoral Team regained the confidence of the teachers in the school. Apparently, for some time the teachers had felt left behind while they watched the rest of the parish ministries flourish. When I reported our progress to Bishop Rodimer, he was affirming and commented, "Finbarr, you surely need a lot of patience as the leader of a vibrant parish."

CHAPTER 11

Growing the Pastoral Team

At the end of summer of 1979 Joe, Ed and I decided to divide the administrative duties among the three of us. Since the citizens of Madison knew Ed the best, he volunteered to act as a liaison between the parish and the city. To our surprise, he volunteered to run as a candidate for the Madison Public School Board.

We were not surprised when he won, nor were the parishioners of St. Vincent Martyr Parish. They trusted him 100%. However, some of Madison's non-Catholics weren't thrilled with Ed's victory. Ed also volunteered to represent the Pastoral Team as moderator of the ladies' Rosary Society chaired by Justine Westhead, a talented and assertive leader.

Since Joe had studied with the Salesian Order, he had better training as a liturgist than did either Ed or me. We asked Joe to manage and schedule all the liturgical services in St. Vincent's Church and in the Italian Chapel on North Street. This assignment meant that he would serve as a liaison with the parish choir, directed by the talented Vicky Martell.

Joe also agreed to oversee all the related activities that took place in the church and the chapel. He would train the male and female altar servers and be a liaison between our team and the church ushers. He would designate which of us would celebrate masses on Sundays and during the week.

Joe made a special appeal to Ed and me that the parish bulletins not be distributed until after mass ended. When parishioners received them before mass, Joe was bothered that some individuals read the bulletin while he preached, which he felt was a distraction. Ed and I just smiled and accepted his request.

When my turn came, I requested that at least one of us visit Morristown Memorial Hospital weekly to give a blessing to our hospitalized parishioners. I offered to be the backup at any time Ed or Joe couldn't make it. I also requested that each week's visitor bring a list of hospitalized parishioners back from the hospital and place it on the notice board outside my office.

Since I had more training as a pre-marriage counselor, I volunteered to create a parish young couples club and to teach Ed and Joe how to form a Pre-Cana program with annual sessions for the engaged couples in the parish. I offered to give the sexuality presentation for any such sessions. My previous experience at the Family Life Bureau had included introducing "Education in Human Sexuality" in 60 or 70 parishes, so I was well prepared for the assignment.

I proposed a new program to help engaged couples better prepare for a lifelong commitment in marriage. Married couples invited by me would invite engaged couples into their homes to discuss their insights about what actions could contribute to mutual growth in the partnership between a couple.

I committed to moderate the Parish Council and invited Joe and Ed to participate in introducing Stewardship into the parish. I also offered to serve as a liaison with the secretarial staff, Phyllis Giannone and Janet Thornton, and with Larry Broullier, the parish janitor and cemetery caretaker

My final suggestion made Ed and Joe smile. "Since I am a trained pre-marriage counselor, I would be happy to help if either of you runs into a serious problem with an engaged couple. I can sit in quietly during the interview and tell you later what I think about the couple's readiness for a lifelong commitment." They both nodded acceptances.

Having laid the groundwork for our work as a team, I obtained permission from Ed and Joe to invite Father Lasch and Sister Marie Schultejann to attend our next weekly meeting as potential consultants for our efforts at St. Vincent's. Our goal was that the right consultants could help our Pastoral Team develop our skills for creating a Post-Vatican Council II parish in Madison. All three of us were familiar with Father Lasch. In the past he had served as assistant Chancellor in the diocesan chancery office in Paterson, NJ. We were meeting Sister Marie for the first time.

As Father and Sister Marie entered the room with me, Ed and Joe greeted them warmly. Prior to the meeting, I had asked Ed and Joe to be open about their assessment of their first months under my leadership.

Ed excitedly initiated the discussion, saying, "Joe knew Finbarr for a few years as director of the Family Life Bureau and as a therapist for priests and nuns. I feel it was easier for him than for me to accept the concept of a Pastoral Team. For the first time in my priesthood I feel accepted as an adult and not the young lad called 'Eddie.' I studied theology in Rome during Vatican Council II, so I am familiar with how the council changed the definition of the Church to include all baptized people as the 'People of God.' I have been working in this parish for over five years and know many of the parishioners and their professional backgrounds, I feel I can be a big help to Finbarr and Joe by inviting lay people in the parish to participate as leaders in the Pastoral Team."

Joe smiled and explained to our guests how we had divided the responsibilities to the parish. He said, "I am excited about managing all the liturgical functions in the parish. I didn't have this responsibility in my previous parish appointments. Because the bishop appointed them, the previous pastors decided to retain that responsibility. Both Finbarr and Ed recognize that my training as a Salesian makes me better qualified to define good liturgical ceremonies and to engage both young people and adults. I can choose relevant homilies as well as the appropriate hymns to match the liturgical calendar. I feel blessed that we have the best choir director in the whole diocese. I know that, working with her, we can add several new choirs, including a children's choir."

Father Lasch and Sister Marie joined Ed and me in applauding Joe's very positive report. I said, "It is hard for me to top that presentation." I added, "I have to confess (so to speak) that I am very lucky to have two associates willing to join me in creating a spiritual family from a traditional parish. I cannot wait to see what happens in the next few months. Ed plans make a list of names of potential leaders for the parish council who will join us in introducing Stewardship to the parish community. He has already suggested two new trustees. I've met them and was very impressed. Both are experienced in the financial world."

I added, "A good friend here in the parish, Carl Vitolo, is familiar with Stewardship and has an Episcopalian friend, a pastor in New York City, who is prepared to visit us and share his experience in helping introduce Stewardship to a parish council."

Both Father Lasch and Sister Marie complimented the three of us on our progress to date. Sister Marie then added, "Fathers, you should be very happy that the Holy Father has designated 1980 as 'The Year of the Family' to be celebrated worldwide. Celebrating the different family cultures within this parish will fit in with your plans."

I replied, "Thank you Sister Marie, you are reading my mind. While we haven't made any specific plans or schedule yet, I expect that we will begin by celebrating the Italian culture first, since about 40%

of the parishioners are either born in Italy or are of Italian descent. Perhaps you'll pray for some good Irish luck for me, especially for when I try to speak Italian with my Irish brogue."

CHAPTER 12

Developing Youth Ministry

Saint Catherine of Siena was born during the plague in Siena, Italy on March 25, 1347, the 25th child to her mother. As a young girl she had mystical experiences along with being recognized as having one of the most brilliant theological minds of her day. She had proclaimed, "If you are what you should be, you will set the whole world on fire."

Like any organization experiencing renewal, St. Vincent's kept growing week by week. While waiting to execute the door-to-door campaign that requested parishioners to pledge 5% of their income to the parish, the trustees gave permission to the pastoral team to hire a full-time youth minister.

When I interviewed Livvy Dinneen, a young mother in January 1981, to become the first full time Youth Minister and a member of the pastoral team, she reminded me of Saint Catherine of Siena. Livvy was a very focused professional, determined to create a community of faith for the teenagers from the local public high-school who attended Saint Vincent's Church. She had a B.A. in sociology and social work from Syracuse University. At the time of the interview, she was earning a master's degree in divinity from Drew University paired with a master's degree in social work from Rutgers. She was also pursuing certification as a youth minister in the Diocese of Paterson and working with youth in her own parish of Corpus Christi in Chatham.

Very impressed with her resume, I asked, "What attracted you to work with adolescents?"

She answered without hesitation. "Adolescents are individuals who struggle to grow and search for meaning in their lives. They need to be guided and loved as they try to find out who they are and how they become fulfilled in this world."

"How do you plan to achieve this as youth minister at St. Vincent's?" I asked.

"I hope to offer them a valid experience in faith by their discovery of what God and religion have to offer. I feel this can be done by forming a community of faith that consist of young people, adults and clergy ministering to each other, by which they can experience caring, listening, questioning and celebrating."

Later she reported how she had honed her skills working with a group called Parents Anonymous, which aided parents who abused their children. In 1979 VAC (Volunteer Air Corps) had cited her for her work with the parents' group.

I knew from that interview that she had the potential to become the best Youth Minister in the Diocese of Paterson. I was extremely excited about my interview with Livvy and couldn't wait to share the news with Ed and Joe. Joe could tell by my actions at the dinner table that something exciting had happened. I couldn't even wait until Theresa had served her usual delicious dinner. I skipped my usual blessing of the food and said, "Congratulations Joe! Thanks to you we not only have the best cook in the whole diocese, but we now will also have the best youth minister in the diocese."

"You are welcome boss," he said with a big grin.

Just as Saint Catherine professed, Livvy knew from day one in Saint Vincent's Parish who she should be as a youth minister and an active member of Saint Vincent's pastoral team. She was prepared to join us setting Saint Vincent's parish on fire!

With input from Father Joe and assistance from Ann Marie Gisoldi, a teacher at Saint Vincent's School, she began her ministry to sixty public school students from Madison high school, who attended our church. Her goal was to create a team of advisors both lay and clerical. Father David Cappola, a talented musician, volunteered to join the team to help the students grow both spiritually and liturgically.

Even though Livvy was the youngest member of the pastoral team, she was very comfortable supporting Sister Alicia, the school principle, when she requested help from the pastoral team on the decreasing enrollment in Saint Vincent's grammar school. Livvy's experience working with Parents Anonymous and the teenagers in her home parish of Corpus Christi in Chatham Township gave her self-confidence beyond her years.

At one of our team meetings, she addressed Father Joe, "Since you are in charge of liturgical programs and assign Fathers Finbarr and Ed to say masses on Sundays and weekdays, do you have any problem with me having a special youth liturgy and program once a month on a Sunday afternoon for my teenagers?"

Joe smiled and said, "I have no problem with that, as long as you are not attempting to celebrate the mass." To which Livvy said, "I would like you to be the celebrant on the evenings that Father Cappola is not available."

"That's fine with me Livvy."

Both Fathers Ed and Joe helped Livvy to get both male and female volunteers to teach her students on the other Sunday evenings.

She got a good laugh from the team when she said, "Some of the students are still talking about their new pastor, Father Corr, and his presentation on sex when he joined the parish two years ago."

Livvy and her committee introduced the Search program, which is recognized by Kendall Bronk, a leading researcher on youth development, because of its effectiveness in creating a vision bigger than self that helps the teenager to embark on a voyage of discovering one's purpose in life. Livvy reported to me and the pastoral team that this program helped the teenagers make a commitment to growth in their faith and dedicated commitment to wholesome living.

The part of this program that was exciting for me was that the teenagers in the program at Saint Vincent's went back to their colleagues at Madison High and invited them to become active in our youth ministry program.

The next program that was initiated was the Antioch Retreat. It was a retreat experience for students in the 10th through 12th grade. Students who made application to join got a letter that said, "We are excited that you are considering joining us for an Antioch Weekend. Antioch is where the Disciples of Jesus were first called Christians. You will be joining teenagers across the world who are searching to develop a deeper understanding of their faith and what is necessary to be a Christian in today's world. The Antioch theme is "With God, all things are possible" (Mt. 19:26)

The Antioch Retreat was originally used by Livvy and her team for Junior and Senior high school students, while Alpha was designed to engage freshmen and sophomores. The Antioch Retreat included witness talks by teenagers, small group discussions, prayer, singing and community building. Its purpose was to help young people learn about their relationship with family and friends and to renew their faith in Jesus Christ.

As leader of the pastoral team and technically pastor of the parish, I was very happy and supportive of the progress Livvy and her team made in developing a meaningful Youth ministry program. When I was free, I would attend the once a month two-hour program in the church. Father Joe assigned me to celebrate the liturgy two times while Father Cappola led the singing, using his guitar. This once a month program included discussion, dinner and a presentation by one of the teenagers.

At each get together, they had fun, excitement and a prayerful experience. The development of the youth ministry didn't end there. The team chaired by Livvy organized a 24-hour Lock-In at the school gym. The students brought blankets and pillows in order to

Livvy Dinneen

take a nap during the night. Livvy reported back to the pastoral team that during the first of these Lock-Ins one of the adult advisors asked the teenagers what they would like to do as a group now that had developed a relationship with each other.

Livvy Dinneen continued her ministry in Madison for 16 years.

CHAPTER 13

Reviving Saint Vincent Martyr School

While the Youth Ministry was being developed under the dynamic leadership of Livvy Dinneen, the trustees Dick and Frank joined me in creating a team to revive our parish school. Our principal, Ms. Carroll Bennett, had joined the Pastoral Team and reported to us that both she and the teachers were concerned about a decrease of enrollment in the school, while the rest of the parish programs were increasing in attendance at liturgies and social events.

Dick reported, "At one of the Parish Council meetings last Spring several members complained that the subsidy paid for the school was excessive ($165,000 annually)."

Frank asked, "What percentage of the grammar school children in the parish attend our school?" I had to be honest and replied

"Only 1/3 of the grammar age children in the parish attend our school. Ms. Bennett told me recently one of the reasons for the dramatic decrease in the enrollment was that many parents were taking their children out of Saint Vincent's for the 7th and 8th grade with the rationale that Catholic Schools could not compete with the opportunities available in the public school system."

Frank looked at me with a smile, and said, "Father Finbarr, according to the article about you in the Beacon (the diocesan newspaper) in June 1979 you were very successful as a fundraiser and organizing Family Day Rallies at the district and state level. How did you achieve that?"

I laughed back, "It all began as an accident. In 1971 I took a good friend and a possible benefactor out to dinner, planning to ask him for $5,000 to supplement the minimal allowance I got from the Diocesan Chancery office. Before I had a chance to ask him or maybe he knew me well enough to read my mind." He said,

"Finbarr, I have heard from people that you are a first-class therapist. I attended your mass a few times and know you are an engaging preacher." He paused and continued "I don't think you got much training as an administrator." I kept my big mouth shut as Al continued, "Why don't I get a bunch of my golfing buddies at the North Jersey Golf Club to come to your residence, which I know is also your office. I will pick up the tab for the food and wine for the party. My goal is to talk several of the men at the party into joining me in raising money for the Family Life Bureau, leaving you free to counsel your clients and give talks on Marriage and Family Life in the parishes of the diocese. Some of these men are very successful business men and like me would be thrilled to help you develop Family Life programs."

I was shocked and replied to my friend, "Thank you, Al, I do appreciate your kindness as the Diocese only gives me $20,000 per year to run the agency. I also have to ask Bishop Casey for permission since some of your golfing buddies are not Catholic." "Okay, good luck. Since you and the bishop are good friends, I am sure he will go along with our plan," he said.

I called the Chancery Office to make an appointment with the bishop, as I didn't want to discuss this important project over the phone. I told him this offer came from a good friend who I knew since I came from Ireland in 1960. Bishop Casey replied "Finbarr you can do whatever you need to do to help families in the Diocese, as long as you keep the ten command-ments and I am free to fire you, if I wish." He laughed and gave me a congratulatory handshake.

Within two months we formed an independent group called The Family Life Board of Governors and within two years our income was more than $80,000 annually and the Family Life Bureau became a sig-nificant agency in the Diocese of Paterson.

The end of the story is that the Family Life move-ment exploded just like Saint Vincent's Family was exploding financially, spiritually and with your help Dick and Frank administratively.

They both supported me as I used the similar techniques to revive Saint Vincent Martyr School. We selected a group of ten people both men and women from the parish, including Dr. Jack Callan who volunteered to chair the committee. Dr. Callan was a college professor and a successful educator who knew how to facilitate a meeting with Ms. Bennett, Father Charles and I participating. We addressed curriculum issues, public relations, marketing the school and how to increase enrollment.

From the committee's inception Ms. Bennett and the school faculty were very appreciative of our ef-forts and excited about the future of Saint Vincent's

School. For some time, they had been feeling that the school was falling behind, as the rest of the parish ministries flourished.

I gained their confidence over the six years as pastor because they recognized that my love for the children in the school was genuine. Having their trust was essential as the committee and I had to make some tough decisions. For instance, we had to close the eight-grade temporarily, because Dr. Callan said there weren't enough students for socialization. (12 students minimum).

To assist with the marketing during Catholic School Week we invited parents to give witness talks from the pulpit, outlining what a Catholic education meant for their children. We held information nights and open houses. We invited grandparents to come to school for a day.

We got a turkey in the local Stop & Shop store and the children cooked it in our kitchen stove for the grandparent luncheon. The first graders, my favorite class, loved seeing me dressed up in an apron and chef's hat and each wanted to be in a photo with me and the turkey.

Since I wasn't 100% sure of being around Saint Vincent's for the next ten years, with the help of the trustees I took one more step to guarantee the survival of the school. We founded the Saint Vincent Martyr School Foundation to raise at least one million dollars from wills and donations. The intent was that the interest from the endowment would subsidize the school. The project was enjoying a brilliant start when I left the parish in 1988.

Saint Vincent Martyr Parish became a special place where people of many cultures prayed, worked, learned and played together. Like any human family it wasn't perfect. It had many positive qualities: love of good liturgies, a caring attitude towards the poor, a nurturing concern for its priests and a welcoming attitude towards visitors. If any reader wants to choose a parish where their children grow to full maturity as Christian gentlemen and women my advice to register as parishioners of Saint Vincent Martyr and send their children to Saint Vincent's school.

CHAPTER 14

Increasing the Weekly Donations

A t the lunch in New York City, Carl's friend Paul discussed Tithing, the third phase of Stewardship. Paul shared the thoughts of Methodist minister Adam Hamilton. In his book *Enough: Discovering Joy through Simplicity and Generosity*, Hamilton wrote, "Money has great power in all of our lives. Used wisely, it is one key to accomplishing our goals, providing our needs and fulfilling our life purpose."

Hamilton emphasized that the creation of credit cards had changed all that. People's debt soared, saving rates plummeted, and home equity became something to be tapped into and spent, rather than a source of security in retirement. The result of was not greater happiness. Instead it was greater stress and anxiety.

When introducing Tithing to the faithful of St. Vincent's parish, I didn't want to scare people away. I wanted them to discover the joy of giving to worthy causes and serving as a vehicle of God's gifts to people.

St. Vincent's parishioners were accustomed to good liturgies. I had tried hard not to disappoint them. I used a conversational tone, and included personal stories, along with the messages from the day's scripture reading. Frequently parishioners would meet after mass and say, "Father Finbarr, you were talking to me today."

I would smile and say "Okay." I now hoped, as we launched the concept of Tithing, that we could build on the good rapport with the congregation.

Carl and I sat down in my office and created a list of people who were financially literate, sensitive to the financial needs of St. Vincent's, and already committed to volunteering their time and talents. The goal would now be to organize a parish-wide campaign that sought parishioners' commitment to donate a percentage of their incomes to support St. Vincent's.

During our regular pastoral team meeting on Monday, I focused on the topic of Tithing, saying, "In Psalm 24 we read, 'The world and all that is in it belongs to the Lord; the earth and all that lives on it are his.' In Deuteronomy Chapter 8, 17-18 we read, 'You must never think you made yourselves wealthy by your own power and strength. Remember it is the Lord your God who gives you power to become rich. He does it because he is still faithful today to the covenant he made to your ancestors.'"

I continued, "Basically, what the Bible says is a) God owns everything, b) we are all stewards and c) we must manage everything for His glory."

Joe added his thoughts, saying, "This Stewardship program is a new experience for all of us. So far it has been successful in increasing the number of people who have pledged their time and talent to the service of the parish. For us to reach our goal of recreating St. Vincent's as a family we need to double our weekly offerings."

Ed responded," If the two of you are comfortable with this next step and the two new trustees are willing to participate, you can count me in as well."

"Thanks, Ed" I said. "Let's talk about who we should invite to participate in organizing this final phase of Stewardship. I guess I will have to introduce tithing at all the masses on the weekend to get it started."

Joe laughed and said," Finbarr, you had the reputation of being a good fundraiser while you directed the Family Life Bureau. Maybe Rodimer sent you here to St. Vincent's partly to increase the weekly collections."

"Let's leave it at that, Joe." I replied. "The next thing you are going to suggest is that I use my Irish blarney to induce the parishioners to donate five or ten percent of their income to the parish."

Ed interrupted, "Let's get on with selecting the committee. We must put our new trustees Dick and Frank on it, as they manage our finances. I would nominate Larry Whipple. He is not only a lawyer, but he also has the reputation of being helpful to politicians in organizing their campaigns."

"Thanks, Ed. It is helpful to have you on board. You know most of the parishioners and their talents. I nominate Carl Vitolo because he has already helped. I would like to nominate Matt Sitter, but I can't because he is a member of another parish. I also nominate Gerry Gannon. He did a beautiful job organizing the speak-up last year, giving parishioners an opportunity to critique all of us, including yours truly. I also want to add Michael Farrell, an executive with a national insurance company, who not only supported me as the first Irish-born pastor at St. Vincent's, but is also dedicated to seeing St. Vincent's grow as a spiritual family."

Father Joe added his own nominations. "My nominations include Vicky Martell's husband, Tony, Vice President and General Manager of Sony Music Entertainment in New York City and president of CBS International Records of New York. I'd like to have Eileen Crowley Horak, a song leader, join Tony as a team to market the Tithing program." (Later in life, Eileen got her Ph.D. at Union Theological Seminary and now is an author of several books including one on the Catholic Church entitled *We Shall Go Up with People.)*

The three of us on the pastoral team agreed to hold our first meeting on a Sunday afternoon to accommodate Tony Martell, who commuted to New York five days a week. We were surprised when all the nominees turned up at the school auditorium as requested. I arranged to have the three of us on the pastoral team and the two trustees sit at the head of the table.

I opened the meeting with a prayer and continued, "Thank you for coming. I hope you noticed that we picked a Sunday afternoon when the Giants don't have a football game (that got a few laughs). I am grateful to you and all the parishioners for your support of the pastoral team. We are now completing our second year. Thanks to all parishioners who participated in the cultural celebrations of Family Year. The number of volunteers in the parish has tripled since we initiated the first two phases of Stewardship.

I continued, "This afternoon we begin implementing the third and final stage of Stewardship that is Tithing, which means enlisting parishioners to pledge to donate a percentage of their income to the parish." I paused for a moment and added, "Where do we begin?"

There was a moment's silence and then Carl Vitolo replied, "Father, as we've learned, our role as Christians is to be stewards of God's creation because everything belongs to Him. This means that when we give a donation to church we are simply giving back to God."

"Thanks Carl, you do such a good job of explaining it. Maybe you should give the introductory homily at all the masses a couple of weeks from now when we introduce the whole parish family to the concept."

"Thanks for the offer, Father Finbarr. I agree with Father Joe that you have a good record as a fundraiser on the diocesan level. Over the past two years the parishioners here have accepted your leadership and enjoy your sense of humor."

While Carl was speaking, I noticed that the lawyer Larry Whipple was very interested in the conversation and was taking notes. After I thanked Carl for his remarks, I asked, "Larry, do you have any suggestions on how we should proceed with the campaign after I have addressed the parish council, written an article on tithing in the parish bulletin, and preached at all the masses on the weekend?"

Larry and Linda Whipple

"My first thought is that we need a door-to-door campaign to invite all active parishioners to donate at least five per cent of their income to the parish," he said. "If the pastoral team and this committee agree, I can organize this effort according to the political districts within the city of Madison. We can also reach out to parishioners who live in Florham Park or other towns."

While I was surprised at Larry's proposal, I could see affirming nods from the group. I thanked Larry and invited others to respond.

Gerry Gannon said, "I like your proposal, Larry. If everybody agrees with it, I will be happy to help you organize the effort." Mike Farrell raised his hand and said, "I will also help."

Father Joe added, "If we are going to ask a group of parishioners to make home visits, I think we three priests should also participate."

Tony Martell raised his hand and said, "Eileen and I will organize a meeting for everyone who volunteers to visit the 1,000 or more homes. I believe this activity will be a historic moment in the growth of the parish."

CHAPTER 15

Celebrating the Irish on Saint Patrick's Day

The successful celebration of the Italian culture over a weekend in January set the stage for the celebration of the Irish on the following Saint Patrick's Day on March 17.

Since I was the first Irish-born pastor in Madison in one hundred years, the parishioners were expecting something special when the committee met to plan this event as part of Family Year 1980. My two associates on the pastoral team, Fathers Ed and Joe, were very supportive. They teased me about the amount of Guinness it would take to satisfy the four hundred people of Irish descent who we expected to attend the mass in honor of Ireland's patron saint. Those who attended the liturgy were expected to participate in the traditional Corned Beef and Cabbage dinner plus the Irish dancing of jigs and reels in the school auditorium.

I understood Ireland's contribution to the world as both cultural and spiritual. In Legaginney we had a mite-box on the dresser in our kitchen, in which we children put pennies as donations to support the Irish priests and nuns who went to Africa as missionaries to teach the natives about Jesus Christ our savior. I remember that the mite-box had a plastic statue of a black child, who bowed his head as each donation dropped into the box. We kids were moved by the action as our mom told us that the bobbing black child was saying thank you for the donation.

I also remember as an eight-year-old going from house to house selling raffle tickets at three pennies each, to support a missionary priest named "Noogey". My cousins, the Brady family down the road from Legaginney, called me the Noogey Man.

By the time I was ordained a priest in June 1960, I realized that there was hardly a country or an island in the world that had not been visited by an Irish nun, priest or Christian brother.

As I grew older, I became more aware of Ireland's tremendous contributions in the fields of drama and literature. Wikipedia lists more than four hundred Irish poets, highlighting one of my favorites W.B. Yeats. (1865-1939) We Irish are proud of novelists like James Joyce (1882-1941) and enjoy being entertained by plays created by JM Singe (1871-1909) and Brendan Behan. (1923-1964). I would be remiss if I didn't include George Bernard Shaw. (1856-1950) His plays *Caesar and Cleopatra (1901), Major Barbara (1905), and Back to Methuselah (1921)* have been popular over the years.

After I came to the United States I learned Irish music was the foundation of Blue Grass music in the US. Even though I didn't have a good singing voice and couldn't play a musical instrument, I grew up enjoying Irish music, as my Mom entertained us nine children, and played the fiddle or melodeon, during the long winter nights in Legaginney. We didn't have either a radio or television to entertain us in the nineteen forties or fifties.

The challenge facing Gerry Gannon and all of us on the Saint Patrick's Day celebration committee was to make a summary of our legacy and integrate it into a parish celebration for Saint Patrick's Day. I shared with Fathers Ed and Joe at our regular Monday morning meeting how I would like to celebrate the mass on Saint Patrick's Day in Gaelic and use the same homily I used back in 1961 the first Saint Patrick's Day I celebrated after coming to the US as a missionary priest.

With help from my uncle, Father Michael Corr, a retired chaplain from the World War II, I told the congregation at my first parish assignment, Saint Agnes in Paterson New Jersey, that Saint Patrick came to Ireland as a missionary bishop in 432 A.D. He climbed the hill of Tara in County Meath and was confronted by the holy Druid, who questioned what Patrick was doing on that holy ground. Tradition says Saint Patrick looked at the ground and picked up a shamrock and explained to the Druid and his congregation, just as there are three leaves on the shamrock, there are three persons in the one God, Father Son and Holy Ghost (Spirit).

I told the congregation that the second mark of Irish Catholicism is devotion to the mass. Even during the Penal days in Ireland, when the British government controlled the Irish people, forbade them to offer mass publicly, the Catholics insisted on attending mass on Sundays. The mass was celebrated by a priest. He travelled incognito and offered mass on what was called mass-rocks, hidden away from British authorities.

The third mark of the Irish faith is loyalty to the pope, our holy father. They believe that the pope was the successor of Saint Peter, the rock on whom Christ built his church. They accept his infallibility as an article of faith. When Pope John Paul visited Ireland from September 29 to October 1, 1979, more than one million people attended his mass in Phoenix Park, Dublin. Two and a half million attended rallies with Pope John Paul when he visited Drogheda, Clonmacnois, Galway and the Shrine of Our Lady in Knock in County Mayo.

The fourth mark of Irish Catholicism is devotion to Mary, the mother of God. I told Fathers Ed and Joe that the Irish who were born in New Jersey and not Ireland, will be shocked when I tell them the Irish are the only nation in the world that created a unique word for Mary the mother of God. i.e. MUIRE. The result is that no Catholic family in Ireland will christen their daughter Muire.

Since March 17 fell on a Monday we decided to hold the celebration on Saturday evening, beginning with the mass at 5:00 PM. I began the mass with a greeting in Gaelic: *Día is Muire duit* (God and Mary with you.) Those Irish born responded in Gaelic with *Agus Padraig (*and Patrick*)*. Our choir director Vickie Martell organized some Celtic music ending with the traditional Irish Blessing:

> *May the road rise to meet you,*
>
> *May the wind be always at your back*
>
> *May the sun shine warm on your face*

And the rains fall soft on your fields,

And until we meet again,

May God hold you in the palm of His hand.

Father Ed had collected Irish art, Waterford Crystal, Celtic crosses and a picture of the Book of Kells, which is always on display at the University College in Dublin.

The air was electric as we all proceeded to the school auditorium, which the committee decorated with paper shamrocks, and the tricolor (green, white and gold) Irish flag.

My previous pastor, Monsignor Christian Haag from Saint Margaret of Scotland parish in Morristown, surprised me by showing up at the beginning of the dinner. He went to the microphone and shared an Irish joke and told the parishioners how lucky they were to have me as their pastor.

Most of the attendees wore a green sweater or green tie to go with a white shirt. I wore my Irish Aran wool sweater, which is hand knit by women in the west of Ireland. Mine was a gift from my classmate Father Michael Hayes's mother. He was a priest of the Duluth Diocese in Minnesota. I also wore my best dancing shoes, knowing that many of the ladies would expect me to take them out on the dance floor for an Irish waltz.

One of the most active families to provide Irish entertainment for any Irish event was the DePortere family. I believe their Mom, Maureen, was born in Ireland. She had her four sons attend Irish dancing lessons, which they enjoyed doing especially on an evening like this. They were scheduled to perform gigs, reels and hornpipes.

The gregarious mom grabbed me saying, "Father Finbarr, you cannot let the boys down. They need you to make up for the Four Hand Reel. Patrick is hurt."

What I didn't realize until later was that the plot had been set up for a few days. Being a good sport and having had a shot of Irish whiskey at the beginning of the evening that helped kill any inhibitions, I took to the floor. The whole place went wild, as I was struggling to remember how my three sisters and I performed a similar dance on the kitchen floor in Legaginney, as our mom played the violin or melodeon.

The choir especially loved it as they remembered me jokingly saying many times, "I am a dancer not a singer." Judging by the applause and lack of boos, I guess I did well.

Father Joe was a little shocked that I could keep up with the three DePortere boys. Father Ed, who was not a lover of Irish music or dancing had already returned to the rectory.

At nine o'clock the *Biddy Early Band* took over, providing music for both the Irish and those who wanted to be Irish for the one evening. Every other tune the band played was an old time Irish waltz. It seemed to me that every woman who could dance wanted to dance with Father Finbarr. A short play entitled, *A Breach of Promise in County Cork,* ended the evening.

CHAPTER 16

The Parish Survey

We invited 150 parishioners, including representatives of all the different parish organizations, to a covered-dish supper meeting. Each person brought some food for the meal, while members of the Rosary society provided coffee and soda.

Gerry Gannon warmed up the attendees with some comedy. He said, "We are not sure what this pastoral team is up to. They hold secret meetings weekly and don't provide us with any minutes. They have appointed two new trustees and we don't know what is happening to our money."

Several people laughed at this last comment. He paused for a moment and then continued more seriously. "St. Vincent's parish belongs to all of us. I think it is only fair that we all have a say in how it is run and what the goals and objectives are. The pastoral team has asked me to assess where we are as a community of faith before we make plans to move forward. This evening we want to critique five areas of parish life: liturgies, preaching, administration, social ministry, and social life. We want you to be totally honest in your answers. Don't hesitate to be direct. I will provide protective armor for the team, so please don't give an answer that you think they want to hear." That comment drew laughs from everyone.

He concluded his remarks, saying, "Father Finbarr, our new pastor, has talked about St. Vincent Martyr Parish as a family, and I know he means it. This is the first of many family meetings we are going to have as we move forward together."

I was not worried about receiving negative criticisms. I had received plenty of criticism from Catholics United for the Faith (CUF) during the time I was actively involved in introducing Education in Human Sexuality to parishes in the Diocese of Paterson. I am sure several attendees were more worried about how Father Ed and Father Joe would handle negative criticism.

Gerry took each topic separately and asked the attendees to write three things they liked about each one and three things they wanted to see improved. When each topic was finished, he asked each group to prioritize their responses.

The people enjoyed it, and there was much laughing and giggling during this phase of the discussion. When they finished all five topics, he asked the three of us priests to sit on the stage as each table reported back to the group. Most of the feedback was positive. In some cases, there were negative comments. We accepted them graciously and with humor.

One table reported that at times they had difficulty understanding the preacher in church. Everybody laughed. Looking at Ed and Joe, I took the microphone to say, "Obviously, they are referring to you two, talking through your noses and with New Jersey accents. I speak perfect King's English."

The evening was a huge success. The parishioners learned that we could take criticism and that we were not defensive. The three of us felt that this was a necessary step for establishing goals and objectives to meet the needs of the eighteen hundred families.

We brought the results of the survey back to the parish council and published them in the parish bulletin. The openness among the parishioners became contagious. We heard from all kinds of people in the parish, from single adults to widows and widowers asking for help. They all were eager to be part of this new parish family.

I asked the parish council to define St. Vincent Martyr Parish and to create a parish mission statement. Some said that the describing the parish as a family was confusing, as sociologists were more commonly defining a family as a mom, dad and children. The majority wanted a definition that was more inclusive and one that reflected the current feelings of parishioners. Our encouragement that they speak up also revealed that many parishioners were harboring hurts that had existed long before the pastoral team existed.

Fortunately, the parish council came up with an almost perfect mission statement: "The mission of St. Vincent Martyr Parish is to heal and renew the parish family according to God's plan." The parishioners became increasingly enthusiastic as we incorporated this concept into our regular homilies and talks to parish groups. Several new parish organizations took root the following year. We had Youth Ministry, the 30+ Club for single adults, Social Ministry to the Poor, Parish Hospitality, the Young Couples Club and the Pre-Cana Team.

One request we from the original speak-up was, "Why don't we publish the Sunday collection amount each week? Does the parish have a budget? How much money do we need to collect weekly to meet our budget?"

When I talked about money from the pulpit, my body language and stuttering voice signaled that it was not my favorite topic. I felt that people attended church weekly to be nourished spiritually and emotionally, and not to be harangued about how much money to put in the basket. But I did have to talk about it at least once a year.

The parish council and some members of the financial fold were not as enthusiastic and trusting about the planned Tithing fundraising approach. One gentleman proposed borrowing $10,000 each from several wealthy parishioners, making it a tax-deductible donation for them and giving them interest on their loan. The parish council and yours truly rejected it. The gentleman who proposed it was angry and hurtled an insult at me, saying, "Father Finbarr, you may be a great shepherd, but as an administrator you are a zero."

I replied with a little sarcasm in my voice, "Thank you, Dan." What I really wanted to say was "Look here, Sir. You have had 11 jobs in fourteen years. I had my last job for 10 years." This was the first time during my years as pastor of St. Vincent's parish that I had to practice anger management!

The first phase of the Stewardship program had gone very well. I was delighted to see hundreds of people sign up to share their time and talent for one or two of the 70+ needs listed on the commitment cards.

The trustees were a little anxious about the parish coffers; the collections were stuck at just $5,000 per Sunday. They estimated that we had to double the weekly amount if we wanted to meet all the needs we had identified. I asked the trustees for just one year's grace before we launched the Increased Giving Campaign. The ideas about Tithing from Carl's New York contact were quite helpful. Ultimately, almost everyone - the pastoral team, the trustees and 90% of the parish council - expressed faith in the concept and in my leadership.

Meanwhile we celebrated Italian weekend. I understood very little of the Italian homily but could appreciate all the Italian art and paintings on display. The celebrations climaxed with a delicious dinner of veal scaloppini. All of us, including me the Irish pastor, dressed in traditional Italian garb. The school auditorium looked magnificent! The committee co-chaired by Fran Mantone and Gloria Agel had decorated it and transformed it into an Italian villa. The *vino rosso* flowed, and we danced the tarantella until the band wished us *Buona Notte.*

CHAPTER 17

A Door-to Door Campaign

Our trustees, Dick and Frank, became active members of the Stewardship Committee for this final stage, organizing the door-to-door campaign. At our regular monthly meeting, Frank estimated the total goal for the regular collection should be $12,000 weekly, to cover the cost of hiring a full-time youth minister and our commitment to the Social Ministry Committee, helping the poor in Madison and in the Diocese of Paterson.

Dick reported that the Social Ministry Committee, chaired by Sharon Capano, distributed 266 Thanksgiving baskets to the financially needy in Madison and to the Diocese of Paterson. I delivered one of those baskets to the father of a family who lost his job in New York City. I didn't want to embarrass him by having one the parishioners deliver the basket to his family.

We continued to have our Stewardship Committee meet on Sunday afternoons, since Tony Martell was busy on weekdays taking the train to and from New York City. His assistant, Eileen Crowley Horak, was busy organizing a training session for the forty plus volunteers who would be visiting the Catholic households on that special Sunday afternoon in November. She and Tony agreed that the home visitors be given a choice of either visiting Catholic families alone or with a partner.

Tony said, "Since it is part of my responsibility at CBS to train new sales personnel on how to market our business to corporate customers, I will be happy to role play with Fathers Ed and Joe on how to approach the different families in Madison or, as some people like to call it, Rose City." He smiled and added "We don't have to teach Father Finbarr. Apparently, he started being a fundraiser as an eight or nine-year-old back in Ireland."

I interrupted saying "Who told you that?"

He smiled again, "It is not confessional. When you were appointed our pastor over two years ago, your bio in the Beacon said you were an author. I went to Barnes and Noble in New York and bought a copy of your autobiography 'A Kid from Legaginney' and read it on the train coming home to Madison."

I thought to myself, I hope they don't know all the secrets about their new pastor.

The next meeting involved the trustees, my two pastoral team colleagues, Ed and Joe, and Larry Whipple. Larry brought five maps of the Borough of Madison and Florham Park to the meeting.

He began with, "I believe the best way to organize the door-to-door campaign is use the same technique that politicians use when campaigning to become mayor or selectmen in the Borough of Madison. As you already know, Madison is a Borough of New Jersey, governed by a mayor and has a Borough Council, comprising of six elected Council members. As you will see on your maps, I have divided the Borough of Madison into fourteen districts. The politicians use this while campaigning to be elected as members of the Borough Council. Later we can create a model to engage the fifty plus families from Florham Park, who are registered parishioners of Saint Vincent's Parish. I will ask Gerry Gannon, who lives in Florham Park, to coordinate the visits to the homes of these parishioners."

Dick Annese asked, "Since this is our first time organizing such a campaign, do we need permission from the Borough of Madison to conduct it?"

Larry said, "I will take care of it."

Frank Weller offered to help Larry, the parish secretary Phyllis Giannone and the volunteers in the rectory to come up with names and addresses of the Catholic families in each of the 14 districts.

Larry suggested we hold the event on Sunday, November 14, as to not conflict with our national holiday of Thanksgiving on Thursday, November 25.

He said, "I will create the invitation and have Phyllis mail it to sixty of the most recent volunteers, who submitted their names last year, to donate time and talent to the Parish as part of their stewardship commitment."

Father Ed, who was moderator of the Ladies Rosary Society, said he would ask Fran Mantone to have some of the ladies prepare coffee and cake to be distributed to the home visitors in the school auditorium on Sunday the 14th, while Tony Martell and Eileen Crowley Horak were teaching them how to approach the respective families.

Since I was the spiritual leader of Saint Vincent's Parish and shared that leadership with Fathers Ed and Joe, I felt it was my responsibility to set the tone for a successful door-to-door campaign on November 14.

I used the Pastor's column in the weekly parish bulletin and my regular Sunday homily to tell the congregation that God owns everything and we, as his servants, manage it for him. I used a conversational approach to engage the folks in the pews to recognize that God's resources are to be developed through us, the "People of God" to accomplish God's mission.

CHAPTER 18

The Parish Plans a Party

Father Joe told me on Monday morning, as promised, that the Parish Council was determined to have a Silver Jubilee Celebration of my ordination, which included inviting members of my family and close friends from Ireland and England to come over for the celebration.

I actually had more important priorities on my mind and on my calendar, and was more comfortable honoring other priests than being the center of attention myself. High on my to-do list included working with the Young Couples Club to create a pre-marriage program (traditionally called Pre-Cana). Because of my experience creating similar programs during my ten years as director of the Family Bureau and my belief in like-to-like ministry, I knew that young married couples would be more effective as pre-marriage educators than celibate priests like Ed, Joe and myself.

Also, since I was active in the national meetings of Family Life Directors and lay leaders, my reputation in the Family Life movement had spread throughout the Northeast and I had begun getting requests to give workshops for priests and lay people in other northeastern states.

Gloria Agel

In addition, and even closer to home in a way, there were changes underway within the parish pastoral team. Father Ed had confided in me that even though he enjoyed being part of the pastoral team, the weather in New Jersey had a negative effect on his health. He had discussed the problem with his longtime physician in Hawthorne New Jersey. The physician asked, "Father Ed, do you have to remain a priest in New Jersey, or is it possible for you to transfer to Arizona or California?" Ed told me that he had written to a few chancery offices in those states and had received a positive response from a diocese in northern California and had made plans to move there.

"Ed, I will miss you, as will many of the parishioners, who got to know you over the years. The insights you shared at our Monday meetings were valuable and you always gave Joe and me good suggestions for the renewal of the parish."

He said "Thank you, Finbarr, for treating me as an adult."

I was not surprised when Joe then shared with me, "Finbarr, I have great respect for you as a therapist. You helped me overcome many of my hang-ups. While I am still in my forties, I would like to take some courses in psychology and counseling."

"Joe" I replied, "Why don't you start with courses at Seton Hall, as I did. It's more convenient than driving into New York every week and you could start with courses in Pastoral Counseling with Dr. Duffy. I had a very good mentor in Dr. Duffy, who taught me how to actively listen to my clients and, when counseling teenagers, to think of myself as a padded wall, meaning they could bounce anything off me without generating an overly-critical response of their behavior. If the Diocese will not pay for your tuition, I will talk with our parish trustees, Dick and Frank, about paying."

At the same time these changes were happening, I had a traumatic experience on a personal level. Father Dennis Haughney, another Irish- born priest and my soul friend for thirteen years, died suddenly at the age of fifty-five. Bishop Rodimer, who knew Dennis and

I were good friends, invited me to give the eulogy at his funeral. It was a difficult assignment; I struggled with anger and sadness. I was angry because Dennis didn't listen to me when I told him he needed to go to a medical specialist after he had a minor heart attack in my presence two months earlier.

Tears blotted my writing pad as I struggled to prepare a positive homily to reflect his personality and cheerful ministry. I chose the gospel reading of the holy women coming to the tomb to anoint the body of Jesus. I invited the mourners, including Dennis's sixty-one cousins, to join me in rolling back the stone of grief that prevented us from seeing Denis in his new state, enjoying the Beatific Vision in heaven.

My priest support group, *Jesus Caritas,* were shocked to hear that I was feeling shaken and abandoned even while Saint Vincent's Parish was doing so well spiritually, educationally and socially. They had become my second family and helped me see that I was looking for support from them, the St. Vincent Martyr family and friends throughout the tri-county Diocese of Paterson. With their support and to help me recover I wrote an article for the diocesan newspaper *The Beacon*, entitled *Loss of a Soul Friend.* Writing the article was both therapeutic and cathartic, freeing me from the overwhelming loss of Denis.

I learned that could share with these brother priests my human frailties and listen to their stories. We did Centering Prayer together at Bethlehem Center and then returned to our regular assignments, including me going back to rejoin the Saint Vincent's family, that was growing spiritually, educationally and socially.

Frequently I would stop at Saint Vincent's School before going to the rectory. I would get hugs from the first graders and have a brief affirming meeting with the school principal. Some of the teachers were aware of my monthly trips to Bethlehem Center and would tease me saying to the students, "Children look, Father Finbarr has a halo around his head." Ministering to the children helped me cope with the sense of loss I felt not having my own family.

So, when Jack Saueracker, the president of the Parish Council called saying "We would like to celebrate your Silver Jubilee as a priest, since you taught us how to really celebrate. We want it to be a party that everyone - especially you - will remember." I agreed on one condition: that the event be a celebration of all that the parish had achieved together.

The organizing committee proposed that we have a children's celebration in the school on the Friday before the adult celebration on Sunday. The celebration on Sunday would begin with a Noon mass followed by an open house.

The highlight of the jubilee celebration would be the afternoon liturgy on Sunday afternoon with all the "bells and whistles." The festivities would then culminate with a testimonial parish dinner dance on Sunday evening.

I insisted that the cost of the dinner be low enough to allow the average family to participate. As Jack Saueracker requested, I gave him the names of siblings and close friends living in Ireland or England that I would like to invite.

Five families in the parish, including the Farrell family on Niles Ave., offered to host and feed my family and friends, who planned to attend.

My first big surprise was that our old nanny from Legaginney, Mary Beatty, was planning to make the trip. (I was her favorite baby!)

It was all coming together but I was feeling some guilt. It was becoming a time of change - within the pastoral team, within the parish and within myself. A this point in my life and 25 years in the priesthood I, too, was beginning to think more about where I was headed.

At the encouragement of the Bishop and with his support, I had agreed to take a six month sabbatical as part of my jubilee year. It would begin just after the parish celebration and include three months in California at Saint Patrick's Seminary in Menlo Park and three months in Rome at the Casa De Clero, near the Piazza Navona. The capstone would then be a trip to Ireland, with members of the St. Vincent Martyr Parish coming over to then accompany me back to Madison.

CHAPTER 19

The Parish Celebration

As Murphy's Law states, "If anything can go wrong, it will." As we waited for the jubilee celebration, that was certainly true within our growing St. Vincent's family.

Josephine, the quiet and patient secretary who oversaw organizing funerals and coordinated details for the parish cemetery, made the mistake of not telling anyone that a body was lost in the cemetery. The phone rang early on Monday morning. Phyllis buzzed me on the intercom saying, "Father Finbarr, Steven Kelly, the attorney general, wishes to speak to you."

I was a little frightened, but, as usual, tried to be humorous. I responded, "Did your husband turn me in?" (Her husband Jim was a state trooper.)

Phyllis laughed, saying, "Mr. Kelly seems to be calling about the cemetery."

When I picked up the line, Mr. Kelly didn't take time for niceties. He said, "Good morning, Father Corr. A former parishioner of St. Vincent's called us to report that his father's body, which was buried in your cemetery 12 years ago, is missing. His son informed us that the family owned a double plot and that they buried their dad wearing a blue suit and his glasses. When their mom passed on two weeks ago, they asked the funeral service to open the second grave so that their parents would be together for eternity. However, their father's casket wasn't there."

Later, when I expressed my surprise at not knowing to Josephine, she apologized for not informing me. "I am sorry, Father Finbarr," she said. "I didn't want to give you negative news when you are feeling happy and looking forward to your Silver Jubilee."

Fortunately, St. Vincent's honest and faithful gravedigger, Michael, was immediately on the case. He didn't rest until he found the coffin four graves away. Sure enough, when the lid was lifted, there was the deceased dad in his blue suit and still wearing his spectacles – and looking none the worse for 12 years in the grave.

The next day, as the family was burying mom and replanting dad, I apologized and offered sympathy.

I also offered to say the final graveside prayers. The family accepted my expression of sympathy but turned down my prayer offer. The oldest daughter told me sarcastically, "We have our own parish priest. We don't want to trust a priest from St. Vincent's."

Later we discovered that Michael's predecessor, Ernie, was an alcoholic who developed the practice of agreeing to rearrange graves in the cemetery in exchange for a six-pack of beer. Regarding the gentleman in the blue suit, when Ernie was told that the father was buried in the wrong site, he didn't move the body because the ground was frozen and covered with snow. He simply moved the headstone four graves over.

At this point Father Ed had moved to California and Bishop Rodimer had sent Father James Reedy, a former Benedictine monk, to replace him. Father Joe, Father Jim, Sister Alicia, and Livvy Dinneen now served with me on the pastoral team.

At a team meeting one Monday morning, Fathers Joe and Jim proposed that a separate, priest-only jubilee party would avoid overcrowding at the parish celebration. The team agreed and asked me to provide a list of 60 or 70 priests who had supported me during the last 25 years.

I was delighted when 65 priests accepted the invitation. Joe and Jim organized a cocktail party and buffet dinner and Monsignor Joseph Brestel, the Vicar General, was the first to arrive. We were soon joined by one of my predecessors, Father Callaghan, who by then was confined to a wheelchair.

Everybody was having a good time and the party was relatively sane until a "drunk" comedian from another town arrived dressed up in a priestly cassock. He roasted me regarding my foibles, real or imagined, during my 25 years in the priesthood. He finished his roast with "Is it true, Father Finbarr that you taught Dr. Ruth everything she knows about sex?"

The jubilee mass on Sunday was entirely different. The theme was a thank you to the family of St. Vincent's for being an integral part of my life and a celebration of our parish family. Referring to the gospel passage I had chosen, I claimed that any good fruit produced was a result of the congregation's participation in the pruning. I referred to the ongoing pruning I was experiencing as the leader of a pastoral team for a dynamic family like St. Vincent's.

After Holy Communion Father Joe introduced members of my family and read a papal blessing that the committee had requested from the Vatican. He then brought the house down when he said, "I don't know if I can talk about the Pope and Dr. Ruth in the same paragraph, but here she is!" As Dr. Ruth entered, the congregation gave her a rousing reception. It was a very happy moment for all of us, and also a cherished memory for me.

Father Finbarr celebrating his Silver Jubilee with his pastoral team and the parish family

CHAPTER 20

Taking a Temporary Leave

From the Pastor's Column on December 8:

"Mark Twain, upon reading with great surprise his own obituary is said to have replied in a letter to the editor, 'Rumors of my death are greatly exaggerated.'"

That came to mind in the aftermath of the many rumors that had been circulating regarding my planned sabbatical leave from St. Vincent's. i.e. 'He is leaving Saint Vincent's for good' 'He is going to write a book' 'He is being groomed by the bishop for a promotion.'

'He is getting married'. (As if someone would be that foolish to marry me!!) 'He is suffering from incurable cancer and is going away to avoid causing any pain to parishioners.'

Let me put all these rumors to rest at once. I am planning to return to St. Vincent's from my sabbatical on July 31,1986.

Sabbatical is a term more familiar in academic circles than in the Church, though its origins are in the biblical story of creation, 'And on the seventh day God finished His work which he had done, and he rested on the seventh day from all the work which he had done'. (Genesis 2 V2.)

In my case, it's more accurate to speak of a sabbatical as an extended leave for continued education, since my first three months of it will involve an intensive updating in Theology, the New Testament, the Church, Christ, Spirituality, Liturgy, Sacraments, Canon law, Moral theology, Social Justice and Preaching.

My address there from January 21st to April 21st, 1986 will be The Vatican II Institute, St. Patrick's Seminary, 320 Middlefield Road, Menlo Park, CA 94025. My phone number if anyone would care to call me will be 415-325-9122. I will return to St. Vincent's for one week and then go to Rome from May 1 to July 31.

I am most grateful to Bishop Rodimer for the encouragement he gave me in May of this year, on my Silver Jubilee, to take seven months away from parish work for renewal, theological updating and a rounding off my education which, as you are aware, has been slanted to areas of pastoral counseling, Family Life Education and fundraising.

During my luncheon meeting with the bishop, he encouraged me to spend some time in Rome so that I would get a broader view of the Church, than I have experienced working for twenty-five years in the Diocese of Paterson.

Monsignor Joseph Gallo a native of Saint Vincent's Parish, has returned from a similar sabbatical in Rome and found it very enriching.

Thanks again to Bishop Rodimer for appointing a colleague of mine, Monsignor Herbert Tillyer, the Chancellor of the Diocese, to serve as administrator of Saint Vincent's parish in my absence. Msgr. Tillyer was the homilist at my installation mass here at Saint Vincent's in September 1979. I got to know Herbert Tillyer, while he was a seminarian as I was associate pastor with Msgr. Haag in Saint Margaret's parish in Morristown. While he resides here at Saint Vincent's during my sabbatical, he will commute each day to his office in the Diocesan Center in Clifton.

I looked forward to this break with mixed feelings. On the one hand, I feel a need for updating, after working twenty-five years in the field. I know I will come back spiritually renewed with a new zip to serve in the priesthood for twenty-five years in the Diocese of Paterson, with many of those years spent here at Saint Vincent's.

On the other hand, my fear about the sabbatical and being away from the parish for seven months is that I will miss Father Charles, Father Jim, our secretary Phyllis and the staff at Saint Vincent's. I will miss the sick and homebound that I visit monthly, because their love and support have meant a lot to me during the last six and a half years.

You all have my address in California if you wish to write to me. When I get my address in Rome I will send it to Phyllis and she will print it in the parish bulletin.

Just to make sure I am coming back from Rome; Saint Vincent's Travel Club is planning on having a busload of tourists come over to Italy for the last two weeks in July. They haven't confessed yet that they are planning on kidnapping me. The truth is that I will be more than happy to join them on the flight back from Rome on Alitalia on July 31. Please remember me prayerfully during the next seven months."

The pastor's column was well accepted, and I got calls wishing me good luck. One single lady gave me $2,000 in cash. On second thought, I shouldn't have accepted it because she had an ulterior motive!

When my sister Marie, who lived in Carlsbad CA heard about my trip to Saint Patrick's Seminary in Menlo Park she called, saying "Finbarr, why don't you come a few days earlier, visit me your older sister, before you drive north to Menlo Park.?" I must confess that Marie, a former nun, was like a second mother to me, while I attended Legaginney School. I remember showing her my homework when I was in seventh grade. She read it, put on a disgusted face, tore up the page and threw it on the turf fire, saying, "I am not going to let you bring that to Master McCarthy!" Changing the topic, I asked, if her boyfriend Jack would be available to fly to New Jersey and share the driving to California with me. She replied,

"I will ask him." He replied, "I am sorry, but no."

Two weeks after publication of the Pastor's column, I packed my bags, bid Fathers Charles, Jim, our parish secretary Phyllis a tearful good bye and started driving south on the Garden State Highway.

I drove between 250 and 300 miles per day, avoided the big cities like Washington DC, listened to my

Irish tapes and once a day said the Rosary. I didn't feel bored and was just as happy that Marie's boyfriend said "No" to her invitation. I stopped at inexpensive motels, got to bed early and hit the highway early each morning.

I recited the Senility Prayer:

> "God grant me the senility to forget the people I never liked,
>
> The good fortune to bump into the ones I do,
>
> And the eyesight to know the difference."

I called friends of mine from New Jersey, who moved to Atlanta two years earlier and asked them if it was OK to stop by and see them. They were excited to hear my voice and talked me into having dinner with them and sleeping over. I made a similar call later and stopped over night with a family in Texas.

My sister Marie called me and wanted to know when I would arrive in Carlsbad CA. She wanted to have a welcoming party for me on Friday, two days later. I replied "Marie, I won't be there until Sunday. Tomorrow I drive through the desert, which is a little scary, as I have never been in a dessert before, much less drive through it. I don't have any more friends to visit on the way. I promise to get there as soon as I can." "Okay drive carefully."

Driving in the dessert was not as traumatic as I feared. Every few miles I met state troopers, some of whom waved to me. I stopped at motel on the outskirts of the desert. Got up the next morning at 6:00 and drove 300 miles to Carlsbad to receive a warm reception from my sister and her neighbors.

CHAPTER 21

From California Institute to Rome

I had reflected on the Pastoral Team, as I drove from New Jersey to California. I realized that the celebration of the different cultures within the family of Saint Vincent's and hiring a competent youth minister changed the family spirit of Saint Vincent. The six month sabbatical was planned to enrich me spiritually, educationally, liturgically and administratively.

I arrived at Saint Patrick's in Menlo Park on January 21, 1986 along with forty other priests from all over the United States. The director of the Institute, Father Bill, gave us a warm welcome. Comparing this Saint Patrick's to the two other Saint Patrick's I attended in Cavan and Carlow (both in Ireland), this one in Menlo Park got an A+ in my judgment. Father Bill was a warm and sensitive leader. The meals here in Menlo Park were delicious compared to what we were served in both the boarding school in Cavan and the seminary in Carlow.

They teased me for my Irish brogue, as I was the only Irish born among the forty attendees.

Father Bill discussed the schedule at the Institute and shared with the golfers among us his advice to take advantage of the local golf courses. The Institute had acquired a clergy discount.

Smoking was a major problem. The eight of participants who smoked (mine, a pipe) volunteered to sit in the back row of the auditorium where the lectures were being held. Father Bill accepted our proposal.

A priest from Vermont stood up and announced,

"Gentlemen, if any of you smoke I will have to return immediately to Vermont, I am allergic to smoke."

We smokers had no choice; we couldn't smoke inside the seminary. I made a more radical decision, I gave up smoking altogether. A fellow priest at the Institute from New York City, who also smoked pipes, was happy to accept my three pipes, one was a classic a wood-cut pipe.

Father Bill introduced one of the seminary's spiritual directors and told us to make an appointment with him if needed. I took advantage of the offer and found his counsel regarding my continuing to serve in the priesthood (or not) very helpful.

I appreciated all the experts in Theology, Canon Law, Moral Theology, Scripture and Liturgy during our three months in the seminary. One scholar was Father Michael Patella OSB, a professor of the New Testament at Saint John's University in Collegeville. I got some new valuable insights from his lecture on the Gospel of John. I knew that by absorbing all this, would improve my own preaching. I could also share these insights with Fathers Jim and Charles at our regular team meetings on Monday morning.

One of the priest attendees from New Jersey, who I got to know during the three months, volunteered to drive my car back to Madison. I gave him $200 to cover the cost of the gas for the trip. I flew back to Newark airport, and spent a few days at Saint Vincent's before I flew to Rome on April 28.

My arrival at the Eternal City wasn't as joyful as my arrival Saint Patrick's seminary in Menlo Park. I wrote the address, *Casa De Clero*, near the *Piazza Navona* in Rome for the Taxi driver at the airport. He acted as if he knew where to take me. He didn't! The owner of the building where he wanted to drop me off spoke both English and Italian. He gave the taxi driver the correct directions to *Casa De Clero*. I relaxed.

At that moment, I decided to learn Italian during my three months in Rome. My reason for doing this was to better serve the 10% of the Saint Vincent's families who were born in Italy and emigrated to the United States.

The *Casa De Clero* (the clergy house) is situated in the center of Rome, close to the *Piazza Navona* and one mile from the Spanish Steps. I was not the only priest born and raised in Ireland in the Casa De Clero. Eight of the Irish born priests in the Casa got an invitation from Pope John Paul II to concelebrate mass with him in his private chapel. They invited me to join them and I accepted.

The Holy Father was very congenial and had his photographer take a picture of each us with him and receiving a gift of a pair of Rosary Beads. I planned to have the photograph framed and show it to the Parish Council at Saint Vincent's when I returned from Ireland on July 31, 1986.

My first responsibility to myself was to hire a tutor who would teach me Italian. She was a friendly lady in her twenties, who committed to meet me for an hour in the morning twice a week for nine weeks.

I was excited and already looked forward to getting in the pulpit in Saint Vincent's and greeting the congregation with *"Buongiorno"*.

I was also thinking of having my friend Carmela Belfiore translate my Sunday homily into Italian and I would say mass in Italian at the Italian Center on North Street in Madison. I did that on a Sunday morning in August 1986. I spoke slowly on the altar, reading the prayers from an Italian missal. I read Carmella's translation of my homily slowly, making eye contact with the congregation. I sensed that the Italian born in the congregation were amazed and pleased that I, an Irish-born priest, made the effort to speak their native tongue. After mass one of the older ladies greeted me with,

"Tanti Auguri Padre. Tu parla Italiano cum metropolitan accento. I solo Sicilian" (Congratulations Padre, you speak Italian with a metropolitan accent. I am just a Sicilian.)

When I came back home, parish members commented on what a different pastor I had become. My good friend and director of the four parish choirs, Vicky Martell, said,

"Father Finbarr, I congratulate you. You are now the best pastor we ever had at Saint Vincent's."

CHAPTER 22

My Parish Family Meets My Irish Family

As the Silver Jubilee liturgy concluded, the choir sang "I Am Blessed," one of my favorite hymns. I removed my vestments and joined the procession to the school auditorium. I felt loved and pumped with excitement, as if I was walking on water rather than on the schoolyard tarmac.

The committee chose Monsignor Haag, better known to those of us who were his former associate pastors as "Ma" Haag, as the speaker (roaster) at the dinner. He was feeble from the effects of a 1967 rectory fire at St. Margaret's in Morristown, which I also experienced.

When the time came for his speech, Monsignor Haag walked slowly and painfully up the steps to the stage. Those who didn't know him groaned, as if to say, "Couldn't the committee find anybody better than an old cripple to speak at Father Finbarr's Silver Jubilee?"

Those critics changed their tune as he grabbed the microphone and spoke in a deep, stained-glass-window voice. He asked, "Fellow hostages, who would spend $25 to come here to Madison on a beautiful Sunday afternoon unless forced to?" Everybody in the school auditorium howled with laughter.

Monsignor shared humorous stories of our time together. He also spoke briefly about his fall down the stairs during the rectory fire, when Father Richard Oliveira and I had the good luck to be rescued from the second-floor window by the Morristown Fire Department.

He concluded, saying, "I've had 40 assistants, but none of them can match Father Finbarr for hard work and dedication to his mission of caring for people. I have never enjoyed an associate more than he. Unfortunately, some of the things we discussed at the dining room table cannot be repeated here."

He paused as several people giggled. Sharon, one of the outspoken members of the choir, yelled, "Don't stop now, Monsignor. Tell it all!"

I was tempted to interrupt and tell the story about Monsignor's life-changing challenge back when I was his associate. One evening we were gathered around the rectory's dining room table. My fellow associate Father Oliveira and I expressed our worry that Monsignor Haag was still smoking cigarettes against his doctor's wishes. We begged him to stop. He knew we were sincere, but as usual he didn't give in without asking one of us for something in return. After a few minutes he said, "Okay, Finbarr. I will stop smoking if you give up putting half-and-half in your coffee."

I didn't hesitate to accept his challenge. My doctor had just warned me about the state of my health. I pushed my coffee mug into the center of the table and said, "That is the last time I will ever drink coffee with half-and-half-cream in it." I have kept my promise for the last 25 years. Monsignor kept his promise until he was called to eternal life on January 24, 1999.

The Silver Jubilee ceremony was topped off with a delicious meal prepared by Fran Mantone and the ladies of the Rosary Society. Although very happy, I also felt sad that I would soon be saying goodbye to my sister Eilish, her 2 daughters Ann and Eilish junior, my sister in-law Wendy, and Mary Beatty, our aging nanny from Legaginney. They had all come over for the event, but were flying back home across the Atlantic the next day.

Over the next weeks I continued my daily Centering Prayer spiritual discipline in the little chapel. I felt loved, but also apprehensive. Earlier that year I had decided to take a six-month sabbatical to contemplate my future in the priesthood. If I felt I couldn't keep my vow of celibacy, painful though it might be, I would resign and undertake a career as Marriage and Family therapist.

But those thoughts were soon put on temporary hold while parishioners, other friends, and I shared a Silver Jubilee grand finale - a trip to Ireland! This outing was my second Irish tour of duty as a trip leader.

I injected some Irish humor by designating the trip as "The Tour Award Program." The Mary Quinn Award would be for the each day's biggest whiner. It commemorated a woman who had constantly complained on the previous trip. The Murphy Award honored the tour member who purchased the dumbest souvenir.

As a counterbalance, the daily Cinderella Award went to the kindest person on the tour bus. The most humorous granting of that award was to two young ladies on the bus. Realizing that old Mr. Flynn had run out of clean underwear, they had taken his T-shirts and briefs for a good washing at the local laundromat.

We arrived at Shannon airport on a beautiful sunny morning. As we landed I remembered the many rainy mornings on my walks to school back in my youth. A smiling courier named Gerry from the C.I.E. bus company was waiting to welcome us. I wanted him to be comfortable with me, so I greeted him in Gaelic. Together we could play jokes on the visitors from Yankee land.

On our way to Galway we stopped on the west coast to see the Cliffs of Moher, a spectacle of one thousand feet of sheer rock rising straight up out of the Irish Sea. I had arranged a welcoming medieval banquet plus entertainment at the Great Southern Hotel in Galway, including that I persuaded a couple with Irish ancestry to perform an Irish jig with me on the dance floor.

The next morning, after an Irish breakfast of bacon, eggs, black pudding, white pudding and brown wheaten bread, we headed north along the shores of Galway Bay. We stopped in the village of Spiddal, where the Gaelic language is still spoken.

I thanked God for the clear sunny day as we stopped along the way to admire the Aran Islands across the bay. At Connemara, the group were amazed that this unspoiled area with vast stretches of bog land and heather-clad hills had survived without being covered by homes and factories. Movie lovers enjoyed the stop at Cong where the movie *The Quiet Man* was filmed in 1952.

This was my second visit to Our Lady's Shrine in Knock, County Mayo. Tradition has it that 200 years ago the Blessed Virgin Mary appeared there to three little girls. I arranged to offer mass at the shrine's main altar. In my homily I reflected on the value of devotion to Mary, the Mother of God. At the end of the mass, we circled the shrine as we said the Rosary, a devotion that the average pilgrim to Knock performs, often in hope of a miracle.

We left County Mayo, and travelled north to County Sligo, with stops at Tobernault Holy Well and Mass Rock. We crossed the county boundaries into County Donegal. We lunched at the Beleek Pottery factory, where my Yankee guests admired the craftsmanship of the local workers in forming and decorating the clay to produce porcelain masterpieces.

Our next stop was at the popular seaside resort Bundoran, the site of the Great Northern Hotel, where my uncle Father Lawrence Corr and his priest friends visited for two weeks of golf by the sea. I had brought a few of golf clubs with me, so I persuaded three of my tour companions to join me for nine holes.

Our schedule called for us to drive all the way from Donegal to Dublin, a four-hour drive. Our tour guide Gerry and "yours truly" entertained the guests on the bus with stories from our own humorous experiences growing up in Ireland After two hours of spontaneous comedy a lady seated in the back of the bus yelled, "Would you two gentlemen give us a break? My sides hurt too much from laughing."

After a good night's sleep in our Dublin hotel, we drove north to Cavan, my county of birth. My sisters Eilish and Dympna and my brothers Colm and Fonsie had arranged for me to celebrate a final jubilee mass at lakeside beside the Park Hotel Virginia. My old friend Kathleen Caffrey from Oldcastle County Meath led the congregation in singing "Amazing Grace," a hymn I love.

My baby brother Fonsie served as master of ceremonies at the event's buffet dinner. He encouraged everyone there - the parishioners from St. Vincent's as well as my forty or so friends, many of whom had travelled from far corners of Ireland to attend the party - to join him in roasting me.

The next morning one of the octogenarians on the tour was slow to board the bus. Her older girl friend asked, "Maggie, what's up?"

She said, "I cannot get my butt on the bus. We were out too late last night with that party animal Finbarr."

For me, the tour and the Silver Jubilee events filled me with gratitude for the many families – my birth family, my St. Vincent's family, and others - who had come together to express their love and appreciation. As the old Irish proverb says, "for wealth is family – family is wealth."